Scale How
MEDITATIONS

Dominus Illuminatio Mea

Charlotte M. Mason

Annotations by
Benjamin E. Bernier, Ph.D.

Scale How 'Meditations'
By Charlotte M. Mason

Introduction and Annotations
by Benjamin E. Bernier, Ph.D.

Published by Lulu.com
ISBN: 978-1-257-85627-5

PREFACE

SCALE HOW 'MEDITATIONS'
Dominus Illuminatio Mea

"This duty of devout meditation seems to me the most important part of the preparation of the mother or other teacher who would instruct children in the things of the Divine life." Charlotte M. Mason.

The series of *Scale How*[1] *'Meditations'* comprise a verse by verse commentary on the first seven chapters of the Gospel according to St. John delivered as Sunday talks by Charlotte Mason to her disciples at the *House of Education,* and mailed to subscribers during the year 1898.

These meditations are important not only for their intrinsic devotional value but also because they offer direct insights into the sources of Mason's theological convictions and the meditative process by which she nourished her personal faith and that of her students. In fact Mason wanted each one of her disciples to understand, practice and teach others to practice, this same devotional discipline so influential and formative in her own life.

Mason firmly believed that education is divine. Education is a matter of the Spirit. In her view there is no difference between Christian and secular education for true education is the same for all, giving a person the opportunity to learn and enjoy the best in

---

[1] "Scale How" was the name of Charlotte Mason's House in Ambleside where she established her *House of Education.*

all things for the glory of God, who is the ultimate source and goal of all knowledge.

For this reason Mason taught her disciples of *The House of Education,* and is willing to teach us and all who would listen, that Christian Education is simply impossible without the regular practice of meditation upon the Word of God, who is Christ, received as the foundation of all life giving knowledge.

TABLE OF CONTENTS

INTRODUCTION

"What is the fitting meat for the mind?" Mason declared at the end of her career that this was the driving question leading her fifty years long educational labours.[2] This question presupposes a view about the nature of a person, the world and God which has become far removed from anything we associate today with education. Modern education has been developed upon the foundations of experimental psychology with its presupposition that humans have no soul and no real capacity for self-determination. In this view only that which is measurable and suitable for standardization may become the proper study of science and in consequence of a scientifically sound basis for education.

It may come as a surprise to some Christian educators that the main ideas we commonly associate with schooling, teaching and learning have been developed upon the basis of such philosophical materialism, but this knowledge helps to understand the gap we often experience between the world-view springing from Scripture and that which now permeates our society and culture.

This is perhaps the main reason that attracted me to the reading and study of Mason's work in my own search for ways to bridge that gap between the truth of Scripture and the rest of all knowledge. It was refreshing for me to learn that Mason's thought was developed upon the basis of a previous school of British psychology which strongly opposed the materialistic reductionism of what would become experimental psychology and defended the spirit of man as a valid category, recognizing its power of self-determination as an efficient force acting over matter even if how this happens may remain inscrutable for us.

Mason made the principle "Children are Persons" the starting

---

[2] Chalotte M. Mason, "Essay Towards a Philosophy of Education" *Home Education Series* 6 (1923): 24.

point of her educational philosophy. But, a person is a mystery to us. How can a suitable education be built upon such a mysterious foundation as that of the immeasurable nature of a person? In order to answer this difficulty Mason appropriated and expanded upon a metaphor rooted on the teaching of Christ and expanded by the historical teaching of the Christian church, identifying Christ as the Word of God which alone can feed the ultimate needs of the human heart. This sacramental analogy between spiritual and material nourishment lies at the heart of Mason's emphasis upon the practice of meditation understood within the Christian tradition of teaching and learning.

In a lecture presented on October 19th, 1886, "Geography as a means of Culture" Mason observed that:

> The mind has its appropriate and necessary food, just as truly as the body.[3]

This implies that not all information is appropriate or necessary for the soul. In fact it is possible to fill the mind with information without actually feeding it. For Mason the question of the proper nourishment for the human soul is of primary importance for education, because "The mind of the man grows upon the idea he receives, as his body grows on his daily bread."[4] This belief is founded upon the presupposition that humans have been created with a natural appetite for knowledge apt to nourish their souls in an analogous way to that appetite by which we identify what is good for the nourishment of the body.

This metaphor serves to illustrate the conceptual origin of the language Mason adopted in reference to what she called 'living books' and a 'living education'. These would be the sort of books and that sort of education by which the mind and spirit receive

---

[3] Mason, "Geography as a Means of Culture" *London Journal of Education* 9 (April 1, 1887): 170.

[4] Mason, "Geography as a Means of Culture" (1887): 171.

the spiritual ideas able to properly nourish its life, which encompasses the whole spiritual, mental, moral and physical aspects of a person's life.

There is yet one next step necessary to understand Mason's emphasis on meditation, which becomes clearer as one proceeds to read the following pages. All living ideas come from the same source, and that is the spiritual source which Scripture identifies as the Word of God, the truth, the life and the way. Therefore, among all nourishing ideas none is more important for the heart of man than the intimate personal knowledge and communion with that Word, who is Christ the Son, God incarnate.

This conviction lead Mason to lay strong emphasis upon the teaching of the Gospels and the disciplines of prayer, Bible reading and, if knowledge is going to be fruitfully apprehended, their necessary complement of meditation. This practice is therefore of paramount importance in the life of all persons, both teachers and learners.

The child is born with a natural appetite for knowledge. "The teacher who has ideas must needs impart them, and to do so takes no more extra time than it takes for the sun to shine." But in order to gain a store of living ideas teachers must lay themselves open to search and assimilate them by means of personal meditation, which is to the mind as digestion is to the body.

The fundamental unity of all truth and all knowledge based upon the truth's spiritual foundation necessary for the learning process explains how the very principles which make a Geography lesson of living interest are the same principles at work in the process of assimilation of the spiritual truths by which human beings are called to live by in the Gospel.

Our separation of sacred and secular knowledge prevents us from appreciating the importance of the sacramental harmony existing between matter and spirit underlying Mason's educational views.

The reading of the following meditations will help us understand why Mason said that:

> This duty of devout meditation seems to me the most important part of the preparation of the mother or other teacher who would instruct children in the things of the Divine life.[5]

Moreover, the following meditations serve to answer one of the primary questions new readers of Mason ask as they ponder the richness of her educational thought: What were Mason's personal religious convictions? What were the sources from which she derived personal inspiration? These questions have received multiple and sometimes contradictory answers. But, in general everyone acknowledges the fact that Mason was a devout, life long member of the Anglican Church and that her adult work was framed against the background provided by the Late-Victorian Church of England ethos. Yet, this leaves a wide range of possibilities in regard to her personal convictions.

In these 'Meditations' Mason presents direct and abundant witness to her personal theological views and the process of interpretation; which has mainly remained under the radar until now. New readers of Mason should know that behind the six volumes of poetry on the life of Christ: "*The Saviour of the World*", which Mason wrote as a devotional commentary on the Gospel for the nourishment of the spiritual life of the teachers and students associated with her movement, lays her life long practice of devotional meditation essential, according to her, for anyone endeavoring to educate children.

This conviction was reflected early in the life of the "*House of*

---

[5] Mason, "Meditation" *The Parents' Review* 17, no. 9 (September 1906): 709.

Education", the teacher training program at Mason's House, "Scale How", in Ambleside within the beautiful Lake District in England. Each Sunday afternoon, since the beginning of the House, after attending the local Anglican Church in the morning, students and teachers would gather in the reading room of *Scale How*; where Mason, or on special occasions other distinguished visitors, would share with them meditations based upon a careful reading of the text of Scripture.

How fortunate would enthusiast of Mason's philosophy would account themselves if they could have a record by which they would be able to sit through one of such meetings and hear Mason herself expounding her ideas on the meaning and application of a text in Scripture!

Well there is good news for all Christian enthusiast of Mason's educational philosophy. During 1898 Mason made an attempt to promote the practice of meditation, central to the life of her teachers training college, by means of a mail subscription service promoted through *The Parents' Review*. Mason had these lectures transcribed and mailed to subscribers as a way to share the content of these mediations in order to stimulate their interest inviting them to follow her example.

We are fortunate to have a collection of that whole year's meditation series as they were mailed from a bounded collection belonging to Elsie Kitching, Mason's personal secretary, a copy of which forms parts of Mason's Archive collection at the Armitt Library in Ambleside.

It was a happy day for me when researching Mason archive I came across this collection of Meditations, entitled 'Scale How Meditations', although it had no identified author. For this reason, at first I was unsure if this collection belonged to the corpus of Mason's writings, but later was able to confirm, by reference to it in *The Parents' Review*, that this collection corresponds with that identified and quoted by Essex Cholmondeley in Mason's biography, where they are referred to as "Meds".

Furthermore, this same whole collection, with some additions, was published from 1906 in *The Parent's Review* providing a permanent public record of Mason's devotional writing in prose, before they found poetical expression in the series *The Saviour of the World*.

This book collects and brings before the general public for the first time the full series of Mason's prose meditations. The main series of the meditations of 1898 on the Gospel according to St. John is preceded by the first announcement in *The Parents' Review* promoting it and the introduction Mason wrote for it in 1906 when the same series was reproduced for the first time in the *Review*.

In order to facilitate the reading of these mediations and to help identify the various sources quoted by Mason, I have included numbered footnotes with short annotations, highlighting the thoughts these meditations suggested to me and providing, when ever I could, the original references Mason quoted to illustrate her teachings. All the footnotes marked by * asterisks correspond to the original footnotes as they were printed by Mason.

I hope that the publication of these meditations will contribute to generate greater attention upon the work and thought of this seminal Anglican Educational reformer and will also edify the lives of children, parents, teachers and pastors as much as it has helped my own spiritual life and the life of my children, family and friends.

> Benjamin E. Bernier
> Corpus Christi, Texas
> February 2011

The "P.R." Letter Bag[6]

Dear Readers.—It has long been our custom here to have a Sunday afternoon reading which we find very helpful, as giving us subjects in common for thought, prayer, and endeavour, increasing our interest in the Bible, enabling us to deal better with the doubts and difficulties which are in the air, and above all, deepening our spiritual life. It is our habit to read through, from Sunday to Sunday, one of the four Gospels, with comments which are more in the nature of a practical meditation than of a lecture or of a lesson. The students who are at work in their various posts miss this weekly stimulus to the higher life; and, in order to help them, some of the students still in training are taking notes so that these weekly "meditations" may be published. Our difficulty is that there are not enough students to pay the rather heavy costs of printing, in addition to those of postage, with out incurring a trying outlay for small incomes. It occurs to me that many mothers might like to share our thoughts from week to week. We find that if there are members enough in our class we shall be able to send out the week's "Meditation," so that it may arrive by the Saturday post, post free, at a cost of one shilling a term for ten weekly papers. I shall be very grateful to any friends who will help

---

[6] This is the first notice of the "Meditations" in *The Parents' Review*, explaining its envisioned purpose and calling for subscriptions. At the end of each edition of *The Parents' Review* there was a section entitled "Letter Bag" in which this announcement was first made. Mason, *The Parents' Review* 8, no. 11 (November 1897): 742.

us in this way. Will they kindly send 1s. with name and address to
Mr. George Middleton, printer, Ambleside, with the least possible
delay. Will the ex-students who wish to subscribe kindly do the
same thing at once. For the future the subscriptions will be
payable on January 15th, and October 1st, when these dates do not
fall on Sunday, and only those members whose subscriptions are
prepaid will receive copies.

Subscriptions sent in now will cover the first term of 1898; but
we ask for names at once, because it will take time to get in the
names of subscribers and to arrange for publication. Hoping for
your always ready help in this matter,

I am, very truly yours,

The Editor[7]
House of Education,
Ambleside

OUR WORK

House of Education: It is gratifying that so many members of the
P.N.E.U. have sent subscriptions for our Sunday "Meditations."
These cannot however be printed unless we have two hundred
subscribers, so we are hoping that many more names will be sent
to Mr. George Middleton, printer, Ambleside, with 1s
subscriptions. Which cover the term beginning on the 15th of
January. The first of the papers will be sent out in the third week
of January.[8]

---

[7] Charlotte M. Mason edited the *Parents' Review* from its creation in
February 1890 until her death in 1923.

[8] Mason, *The Parents' Review* 8, no. 12 (December 1897): 798.

INTRODUCTION TO THE 'MEDITATIONS'
IN THE PARENTS' REVIEW - 1906

Meditation
by the Editor[9]

The preceding article[10] on 'Teaching Children to Pray' suggests, as however unworthy a sequent, a paper on a subject which received more attention in the earlier Christian church than in days when the social outcome of Christianity is apt to stand for Christianity itself. But it cannot be too often repeated that Christianity does not consist solely in good works, nor even in prayer and other devout observances.[11]

---

[9] Mason, "Meditation" *The Parents' Review* 17, no. 9 (September 1906): 707-709.

[10] The Rev. Prebendary J. S. Northcote, "Teaching Children to Pray" *The Parents' Review* 17, no. 9 (September 1906): 699-706.

[11] 'Our children are the children of God, and above all things they must learn to live as children of God, therefore we must take care to train their spiritual faculties: those senses of the soul by which we feel the presence of God, and recognise His claim upon our conduct.

...

They should be advised to choose a collect out of the Prayer Book, and use it every evening for a few weeks, and then to change it for another. Favourite verses out of the Psalms may be treated in the same way—but the boy or girl should choose for themselves. Children should not be taught to say long or many prayers. One short petition for help to resist a special temptation or do some particular thing, if it is thoughtfully said, is quite enough for a morning prayers,

Christianity is not merely the following of Christ, but is chiefly, the knowledge of Christ, to be attained by a constant, devout contemplation of the Divine Life. Hence, the primary importance of meditation to the Christian soul. We cannot grow into the likeness of that which is unknown to us, and we cannot know except by that process of reflective contemplation which we name meditation.

It is told that Mr Romanes[12] once asked Darwin to advise him as to the best course to take in the pursuit of science. The answer of the elder scientist was 'Meditate.' If meditation be the secret of success in the scientific, much more must it be so in the spiritual, life: for, as has been well said by the late Dean Church, the spiritual life must be nourished upon ideas, and not merely emotionally stimulated. We are *transformed by the renewing of our minds*, and with the renewed vigour imparted by 'new thoughts of God,'[13] we are again enabled for the spiritual activities of prayer,

and far better than longer prayers said by rote, because in our prayers we should always think more of what we ought, or ought not to be and to do, than of what we ought to say; the words, whether of a collect or out of our own heads, will always come when we are in earnest about improving our characters or our conduct. In the evening, prayers may be longer, because we can give more time to meditation, and in the evening we ought to think of our faults, for in the Christian life there must always be the battle against sin, we must fight our faults from beginning to end. And we must continually pray for God's help to find and face and conquer them. This is the true purpose of repentance, and the way to work out our own salvation by the Grace of our Lord and Saviour Jesus Christ.' The Rev. Prebendary J. S. Northcote, "Teaching Children to Pray" *The Parents' Review* 17, no. 9 (September 1906): 699, 703-704.

[12] George John Romanes (1848–1894) evolutionary biologist, the youngest of Charles Darwin's academic friends, who laid the foundations of what he called 'comparative psychology' postulating the similarity of cognitive processes and mechanisms between humans and animals.

[13] John Keble, 'Morning' *The Christian Year.* 54.

New mercies, each returning day,
Hover around us while we pray;
New perils past, new sins forgiven,

praise, and godly endeavour.

If we assume that a vigorous Christian life must depend largely on devout meditation, the question arises: How, and how early, may children be led to meditate? All important things are simple, and this question of children's meditations is very simple indeed. The answer depends upon the conduct of the daily Bible lesson. If mother or teacher indulge in much talk, the active principle in the child's mind which generates ideas is deadened —as it were, drowned— and nothing happens beyond the pleased interest of the moment. But suppose the little lesson be conducted something in this way: let the lesson be about Zacchaeus, to children of, say six.

The last lesson will have brought the children to the particular point in the history where the story of Zacchaeus occurs, and the teacher might begin by a few words about Jericho —the trees by the roadside, etc., quite a few words— and then, read to the children the first ten verses of S. John 19, with simplicity, reverence, and a perfect delivery of every word. Hardly any comment will be necessary; a smile perhaps where the little Zacchaeus climbs the tree may help to interpret to the children the kindly humour of our Master. The story read, the children should be allowed to ask questions. They will probably want to know what is meant by 'a publican,' 'a son of Abraham,' and the like. Then they should be called upon to narrate the story, two or three children taking up the narrative in turn.[14] If the reading has been careful and interpretative, it will be found that the children's narration will be almost verbatim. Then the teacher may allow herself in a few comments, just a word or two about the

---

New thoughts of God, new hopes of heaven.

[14] This is the first direct reference to the practice of narration in relation to the discipline of meditation in Mason's published works. It is worth noting that before the 1904 edition of *Home Education* for the Home Education Series it did not contain any section on Narration.

graciousness of our Lord, and the great joy that came to Zacchaeus because he 'wanted to see Jesus.'

But all this is not meditation? No; but at the end, the mother, or teacher, might say, 'You awake sometimes before nurse comes. If you should do so to-morrow, you might tell this story to yourself without leaving out a word.' This is one of the pleasant things a child will love to do; and here we have meditation, not in its initial stage, but in perfection; because this act of mental narration has the curious effect of bringing before the mind's eye the persons and the action of the tale, somewhat as they would appear in a cinematography; and, with the progress of the story and the action of the figures, come into the mind the ideas proper to it —you meditate in the fullest sense of the word.

This manner of meditation might well be recommended to children of all ages; their own evening devotional reading forming the subject of their morning meditation, or *vice versa,* whichever is the more convenient.

About the period of confirmation, perhaps a fuller pondering of these things in their hearts may be recommended to young people, according to their power and inclination for this sort of exercise. I add two or three short meditations which may suggest the sort of thing I have in view. I should like to add that this duty of devout meditation seems to me the most important part of the preparation of the mother or other teacher who would instruct children in the things of the Divine life.

SIMPLICITY

A Bible Study[15]
by Charlotte M. Mason[16]

In the course of our Scale How Bible Readings in St. Luke's
Gospel, we came upon a discourse of our Lord's, so full of
illuminating and connected teaching upon the subject of
Simplicity that it seems well to draw the attention of parents to
the Divine teaching on a quality which is the first condition of all
successful work with children. The simple person can do anything
with a little child; the unsimple loses the key and cannot force an
entrance into a child's heart. When governess or nurse, aunt or
uncle, even mother or father, fails to get hold of children, it is
usually because he or she is a person of unsimple character. Our
Lord, in his amazing discourse, full, as is all his teaching of the
philosophy of life, unfolds to us the nature of simplicity, and
investigates the two causes which hinder men from living simple
lives. We are unsimple, we educators, because we are insincere, or
because we are anxious.

'The *lamp* of the body is the eye' we are told; not 'the *light* of the
body is the eye,' as the Authorised Version has it. Were this the
case we should probably be right in saying that a 'man can but
walk according to his lights,' however dim and illusive these be.
But the eye is the lamp, the horn lantern, through which that light
is to shine whereby the traveller sees his way, or which, when set

---

[15] Mason, *The Parents' Review 9*, no. 1 (January 1898): 46-54. First
Meditation published in *The Parents' Review.*

[16] This Meditation was also republished in *The Parents' Review*, July 1921
and in *The Story of Charlotte Mason*: 275-284.

upon a stand or candlestick—our settled circumstances or condition of life—shows light to those that are in the house. This lamp of the body is our power of spiritual reception and perception, that universal gift of spiritual discernment proceeding from 'the Light that lighteth every man.' We all know that we possess this gift, we say, 'we will look into the matter,' that such a one has power to 'see into things.' When the eye is single, the whole house of many chambers—heart and mind and soul—is full of light. We see our way and walk cheerfully onwards when the horn lantern is 'single,' but if the lantern be of double horn, or if it be cobwebbed, neglected, long disused, the light is dimmed to the point of extinction by the opacity of the lantern. We fail to see by that light which lighteth every man and are at the mercy of every wandering Will o' the wisp of baneful and fitful light. We say of some people that they are perfectly transparent, a good and beautiful thing. We say, everything is clear as day about them. We call them sincere, that is, clear (as honey free from wax). We all value these people 'open as the day.' They are shining as a clear, clean lamp, letting forth light. Do we ask ourselves—Have *we* this single eye? The answer is to be found, not in anxious enquiries into our motives and feelings, but in out-shining of the light in simple, humble, pleasant doing of that duty which comes next. By turning the light upon ourselves we produce dark lanterns. The most profound sense of our own unworthiness, abject humiliation, these are but forms of that self-consciousness which is a turning of the light upon ourselves, and so presenting a dark lantern to the world. We may know when the light shines out, because then we *see* other people. Before, men are to us but 'as trees walking.' It is not only upon our brother that the search-light is cast, for the pure in heart; the single of eye shall see God. The world hungers for the beatific Vision. It would fain satisfy itself with fame, prosperity, human love; but when all these are in possession the desire of men is still towards the vision of God, that final bliss, to be discerned only as we have light, that light shining in darkness and lighting every man which is born into the world, that light of the world Who is our life.[17][18]

Now we have the discourse interrupted. A Pharisee asks our Lord to dine with him. He knew what was in the Pharisees, but we never read of his refusing any invitation. The graciousness of the Divine guest is met in a spirit of carping criticism. He eats with unwashen hands. We wonder at the sudden and terrific burst of the wrath of the Lamb which follows upon the supercilious glances and inward comments of the Pharisees. Why was Christ, who was tender to criminals and patient with sinners, austere and terrible in his denunciations of the Pharisees? We understand better when we perceive that He is but continuing his discourse on the single and the double lantern, the simple and the unsimple soul. It would be a key to the better understanding of many of Christ's discourses if we perceived that He works out a single train of thought exhaustively in the face of many interruptions, frequently using these very interruptions to demonstrate his meaning. Our Lord would show what the simple soul is by this present example of the unsimple. These men were the religious formalists of their day. Doubtless they believed that they were the upholders of religion, the witnesses for the honour of Jehovah. Now the whole point of the invective lies in the fact that they believed these things, believed in the sincerity of their own lives and, yet, they are branded as hypocrites. Conviction was impossible to them, so double were their thoughts. So they began to press upon him vehemently and to provoke Him to speak of many tings, laying wait for Him, to catch something out of his mouth. Upon this day was driven in another of the nails upon which Christ hung upon the Cross.[19]

---

[17] Notes identified by arterisks (*) were part of the original printout mailed weekly by Charlotte Mason to subscribers during the year 1898. These were collected and bounded by Elsie Kitching for her own personal use. This bounded copy is currently part of the collection of books belonging to Mason at the Armitt Archive, Ambleside.

* St. Luke 11:33-37.

And now the 'many thousands of the multitude trode one upon another to hear Him, and He began to say unto his disciples first of all, Beware ye of the leaven of the Pharisees, which is hypocrisy.' This would be startling. We can imagine that a feeling of complacency might have stolen into the hearts of the disciples. Anyway they were not hypocrites, whatever were their faults, that was not one. But they have not escaped. Christ bids *them* beware, be aware of this leaven of hypocrisy; they had heard Him speak before of leaven, they knew very well that "a little leaven leaveneth the whole lump," that leaven permeates the whole loaf through and through and cannot, by any human process, be separated form the bread; and they whom Christ calls in this very connection "my friends" are warned to be aware of the possibility of this leaven of hypocrisy in themselves. The very complacency with which they had possibly listened to the exposure of the Pharisees may have called down on them this more gentle rebuke. But how could they who had given up all and followed Christ yet be hypocrites? Alas, the danger of this damnable state, this eternal death of hypocrisy, lies in its insidiousness. Our rude modern notion of hypocrisy makes it the sin most easily to be avoided, most contemptible in the eyes of those who call themselves the 'friends' of Christ. The hypocrite, in our view, is the man who makes believe in the eyes of others to be that what he is not; but our Lord flashes a searching light upon his friends and upon his enemies and shows in a way never to be forgotten that the leaven to beware of is the posing before the eyes of our own consciousness, making believe to ourselves to be that which we are not. The all-penetrating leaven is that which we call insincerity; insincerity as to what we are, what we think, what we purpose, which is, alas, 'the natural fault and corruption of the nature of every man,'[20] unless as he is illuminated by the Light of

---

* St. Luke 11:37-54.

[20] This is the language of the *39 Articles of Religion*, the doctrinal statement of the Church of England resulting from the sixteenth century reformation, in

the world.

This warning is supported by three arguments. First, our inmost thoughts are and shall be known in this world as well as in the next. It is vain to make ourselves believe that we are other or better than we are, because neither God nor man is deceived, we alone are the victims of our own delusion. Next, why should we compromise and commit ourselves and make believe to be other than we are for the sake of any risk to our worldly well-being when the loss of life itself is not the great and final thing we think it is. Do not thousands of men, firemen, soldiers, miners and the like, face death daily in the simple doing of their duty to earn their daily bread? Why should any fear of consequences lead to disingenuous lives? And lastly, what cause have we for subterfuges when this life itself is in the care of God and the very hairs of our head are numbered. There is but one thing to fear, and that is the state of the hypocrite, the soul leavened with insincerity, which is the hell of the spirit here and, conceivable, hereafter. The insincere, the self-conscious, the self-regardful, these are they who do not confess Christ, who have reason to fear the condemnation of 'I never knew you.'[21]

Continuing his investigation of the subject of the single eye, or,

---

relation to the doctrine of original sin: *Article IX. Of Original or Birth-Sin:*

"Original sin standeth not in the following of Adam, (as the Pelagians do vainly talk;) but it is the fault and corruption of the Nature of every man, that naturally is engendered of the offspring of Adam; whereby man is very far gone from original righteousness, and is of his own nature inclined to evil, so that the flesh lusteth always contrary to the Spirit; and therefore in every person born into this world, it deserveth God's wrath and damnation. And this infection of nature doth remain, yea in them that are regenerated; whereby the lust of the flesh, called in Greek, *phronema sarkos*, (which some do expound the wisdom, some sensuality, some the affection, some the desire, of the flesh), is not subject to the Law of God. And although there is no condemnation for them that believe and are baptized; yet the Apostle doth confess, that concupiscence and lust hath of itself the nature of sin."

* St. Luke 12:1-8., R.V.

as we venture to call it, simplicity, our Lord utters words more marvellous, if possible, more divine, than any others we have on record. It is as if He looked into the hearts of his 'friends' and saw there questionings as to his wisdom in thus outraging the powerful Pharisee; as if He looked on further and saw the doubt of Thomas, the denial of Peter, and gazing still beyond the present multitude, down the ages of the church's history saw the anguish of perplexity which Huxley[22] expresses in the words, 'I had and have the firmest conviction that I never left the *verace via*, the straight road, and that this road led nowhere else but into the dark depths of a wild and tangled forest.' Looking forth upon this dark and tempestuous sea of doubt, whose billows have beaten against the foundations of the Church from that day unto this,

---

[22] Professor Thomas H. Huxley, who coined the term 'agnostic'. The preceeding context to Mason's quote explains his position: "When I reached intellectual maturity and began to ask myself whether I was an atheist, a theist, or a pantheist; a materialist or an idealist; a Christian or a freethinker; I found that the more I learned and reflected, the less ready was the answer; until, at last, I came to the conclusion that I had neither art nor part with any of these denominations, except the last. The one thing in which most of these good people were agreed was the one thing in which I differed from them. They were quite sure they had attained a certain 'gnosis,'—had, more or less successfully, solved the problem of existence; while I was quite sure I had not, and had a pretty strong conviction that the problem was insoluble. And, with Hume and Kant on my side, I could not think myself presumptuous in holding fast by that opinion. Like Dante,

> Nel mezzo del cammiu di nostra vita
> Mi ritrovai per una selva oscura,
>
> [In the midway of this mortal life,
> I found me in a gloomy wood astray.]

but, unlike Dante, I cannot add,

> Che la diritta via era smarrita.
> [Gone from the path direct.]

On the contrary, I had, and have, the firmest conviction..." Thomas H. Huxley "Agnosticism" *The Nineteenth Century* 25 (February, 1889): 182-183.

Christ says, 'every one who shall speak a word against the Son of Man'—We feel the trepidation of the disciples, such a terror of failure as came upon them later when each asked, 'Lord, is it I?' Thought is quick and there were no doubt searchings of heart in the very space of time it took to complete this majestic utterance. There is profound anxiety amongst them as to whether they are fulfilling their relation to the Son of Man. We all know the pang of a sudden conviction of failure in our relations with our closest friends, but 'We needs must love the highest when we see it,'[23] and what other treachery can equal this of speaking words against the Son of Man! Our Lord saw, we may believe, quailing of heart in his disciples, and the anguish of doubt in thousands who have denied Him since; and He ends his sentence with the most divine of all utterances, equalled only by that word on the cross,—'Father, forgive them, for they know not what they do'—'whoso shall speak a word against the son of Man *it shall be forgiven Him.*' Think of the thousands who to-day are, let us not say lost, but bewildered 'in sinless gulfs of doubt.' Such men are often our teachers; they have learned form above many things for our profit. They often lead lives of purity and beauty; but they have no place for Christ. We look on and are not puzzled. We know that their wisdom and goodness also come from the Light which lighteth every man. We know that the words they speak against the son of Man are forgiven; and we feel some faint touch of the divine compassion that they should be constrained to utter words of such infinite pathos as these:—"Though I have found lions and leopards in the path; thought I have made abundant acquaintance with the

---

[23] Lord Alfred Tennyson, "Guinevere"

... Ah my God,
What might I not have made of thy fair world,
Had I but loved thy highest creature here?
It was my duty to have loved the highest:
It surely was my profit had I known:
It would have been my pleasure had I seen.
We needs must love the highest when we see it,

hungry wolf, that 'with privy paw devours apace and nothing said,' as another great poet says of the ravening beast: and thought no friendly spectre has even yet offered his guidance, I was, and am minded to go straight on until I come out either on the other side of the wood, or find there is no other side to it, at least, none attainable by me."[24] This will be forgiven, let us remember, to those who walk by means of the Light, but do not see it. For ourselves, let us rather bear in mind that we each carry that which is as priceless to a Christian as is her honour to a woman. Let us treasure our loyalty as our life, remembering it is the one jewel which a subject has to offer to this king. 'Loyalty forbids,' that old motto of the loyal house of Basingstoke, is the answer to every assault of doubt. The subject who is not loyal is, as a subject, nothing: and this is never so true as when the subject is a Christian and the King is Christ.

Then follows a sentence as tremendous in its condemnation as the last is amazing in its tenderness:— 'Unto him that blasphemeth against the Holy Spirit it shall not be forgiven.' Why this difference in the divine regard of sins that seem to us equal or, if not equal, perhaps we feel that blasphemy against the Holy Ghost is a less extreme offence than blasphemy against the Son of Man? If we consider that our Lord's discourse is not a series of disconnected utterances, but a close reasoned-out and amply illustrated argument based upon the thesis, 'when thine eye is single, thy whole body also is full of light,' we are better able to follow the thought in this most anxious passage. It is perhaps possible to speak words against the Son of Man in sincerity and with a single eye; but blasphemy against the Holy Ghost, that calling of evil, good, and good, evil, of which we read in the previous chapter—when the Pharisees declared that by Beelzebub, the Prince of the devils, He cast out devils—this comes only out of a heart leavened, permeated through and through in all its

---

* Professor Huxley's Article on Agnosticism (Nineteenth Century, February, 1889).

substance, by insincerity, which is hypocrisy. It is not impossible that that quality to which we give the gentle name of tolerance calls for our scrutiny in this regard. Do we say of 'extortioners, unjust, adulterers,' 'Ah, well, the devil is not so black as he is painted; he is a good fellow after all; one might have done worse oneself in his place.' Do we ignore the means by which a man has made wealth and social position for himself, and rest content with the fact that he is wealthy, and able and willing to minister to our pleasure? This is what the world calls tolerance, and it is very like, and yet essentially unlike, the charity of the Gospels. A fair test of the sincerity of this tolerance of ours is our attitude towards people who are fighting strenuously with any one of the evils of the world. Do we speak with heat and contempt of the missionary as a luxurious liver and a tiresome person, who does more harm than good; of the philanthropist as a meddlesome fellow, who cannot let well alone; of the temperance worker as a common sort of person with a crank; and do we say these things without any careful study of the question we thus sum up? If so, it is not impossible that this tolerance of the world, easy towards vice and bitter towards virtuous endeavour, is this very sin of blasphemy against the Holy Ghost. For this sin there is no forgiveness, because there is no place for forgiveness, there is no single spot of the nature in which the leaven does not work—'it leaveneth the whole lump.' There is no hope of reform for the hypocrites who deceive themselves into thinking evil, good, and good, evil, but there is the larger hope—'Ye must be born again.'[25]

Our Lord's thoughts return to the sincere, 'His friends,' and He foresees the suffering, persecution, martyrdom, which has attended them, more or less, through the ages. For all these occasions of distress He gives a single command,—not a counsel, not an entreaty, but a command—'Be not anxious'; and from this point the discourse takes a new note. Our Lord deals with another

---

* St. Luke 12:10-13, R.V.

doubleness of human nature, another cause which militates against the simple life, the plain seeing of the single eye. The object lesson, as usual introduces the teaching. There is a man in the crowd who is anxious. He is suffering, so he thinks, from an injustice. He is anxious to claim his rights. Here is a teacher, who 'spake as man never yet spake,' surely He will see justice done between him and his brother. But, behold, Christ flashes upon him the light of his truth, and what he believed to be the desire for fair play stands revealed to him as covetousness. His anxiety clouds this man's lantern, and he, too, cannot see.

From this point, though the single eye is still the subject under elucidation, the discourse takes a new departure; a new thesis is laid down—'a man's life consisteth not in the abundance of the things which he possesseth'; a new warning is given to those which are his friends—'take heed and keep yourselves from all convetousness.' Then follows the story of the man who had such abundance of things that he had no place for them all. His very abundance was a care to him. Before he could sit at his ease and enjoy, he must build, get room for his belongings. And old Jewish story, perhaps, but never was it more true than to-day 'Things are in the saddle,' as Emerson[26] has well said, and man is the heard-breathed horse under this pitiless rider. We accumulate furnishings and pictures and appurtenance and belongings without end, and we say in vain, 'Soul take thine ease and enjoy

---

[26] Ralph Waldo Emerson, *Ode:*

> The horseman serves the horse,
> The neatherd serves the neat,
> The merchant serves the purse,
> The eater serves his meat;
> 'Tis the day of the chattel,
> Web to weave, and corn to grind;
> Things are in the saddle,
> And ride mankind.

that which thou hast got,' because it is the very nature of this fever of covetousness, this desire for the accumulation of things, that it grows on that upon which it is fed, and each new possession turns on, as it were, a dozen new desires. There is no middle way; only the one counsel will save us,—that we beware of *all* covetousness. It is interesting to observe how many thinkers have reached this conclusion from quite another stand point. Men who begin, not with a thought of obedience to Christ, but with desire to find some panacea for the world's evils, tell us that there is no hope for us until we learn to do without "*things.*" I heard a well known clergyman, who is working in the East End,[27] say, the other day, that if anything could induce him to give up this work, it would be the desire to preach simplicity of life in the West End.[28] Already many people are beginning to ask themselves, not what can we have, but what can we do without. People begin to see that a room, from its very name, implies space, space for people to move in and simple seats, like William Morris' rush–bottomed chairs, for example, where they may sit and talk to one another; places which are cabinets, which are upholsterers' stores, which contain more than space and seats, tables for occasional uses, and a few worthy art objects to satisfy and educate the eye, these should not be called rooms, for that is precisely what they are not. But our Lord does not limit his warning to "things," though he emphasizes these. He bids His 'friends' beware of *all* covetousness, for covetousness begets envy, and envy is as the rottenness of the bones, and the envious are excluded from heavenly places. This is true whether we covet a new gown or a lovely vase, advancement in life or our neighbour's social advantages. Nor is that covetousness of the heart which we call jealousy exculpated. It

---

[27] The "East End" refers to the area of London, which during the 19th Century was characterized by extreme overcrowding and concentration of poor people and immigrants.

[28] In contrast to the "East End" the "West End" was the term used in the early 19th century to describe the fashionable areas of London.

would seem as if our Lord stripped us of the flimsy apron with which we cover the nakedness and poverty of our souls, and shewed us once for all, that much of that which we dignify under the name of anxiety, and pity ourselves for enduring, shews, in the Light of life, as covetousness and of which we must be aware. This is true even when we have wrongs to endure, or when our anxiety is for others. There is no hint that the covetous man preferred a *false* charge against his brother, and it is very possible that wife and children were objects of his care. Even so searching is the word of God.[29]

There are few things more gratifying than to perceive that the mind of the son of Man worked as our minds work, that a subject develops in his thought according as it would do in our own. And now we come to another such exquisite gratification; we perceive that the Son of Man is a poet also; and is there a poem in all the world which so fulfils all the functions of poetry, which is so full of sweetness, refreshment, rest, illumination expansion, as that poem which bids us 'consider the lilies of the field,' and 'the fowls of the air.' All poets see and know, and inasmuch as He sees with an unbounded vision, sees all the past and all the future and all the issues of life, how could our Lord not be a poet? These words are so dear to us all that it is hardly necessary to dwell on them. But see how large is the Divine thought. Beauty should go beautifully, and it is with grace and fitness as the lilies of the field—possibly the red anemones of southern Europe and Palestine—that our Lord would garb the human form divine. And for meat, how well for the birds who have a table ever spread with the food of their desire; and in this lavish and gracious measure, our Father knoweth that we have need of these 'things.' How well the apostrophe fits our anxious hearts—'O, ye of little faith.' that is just it; we are not without faith, but we have so little, and the 'doubtful' mind expresses our state so precisely. We *may* not be of

---

* St. Luke 12:13-21.

doubtful mind, we *may* not be anxious, for this also is a form of insincerity and obscures the light of the Christian soul whose business it is to shine. Education is an atmosphere, and nowhere else do we get the atmospheric conditions proper for the living soul set before us in a manner so exhaustive, as in this discourse of the Son of Man.[30]

Meditations.—We still must beg our readers to subscribe for the 'Meditations.' We must have more members or we cannot afford to have them printed. Our readers will perceive that we have tried to 'catch them with guile,' by publishing the substance of two or three "Meditations" as an article under the heading of *Simplicity*.[31]

---

* St. Luke 12:21-31., R.V.

[31] Mason, "Our Work" *The Parents' Review 9*, no. 1 (January 1898): 55.

SCALE HOW 'MEDITATIONS'

Dominus Illuminatio Mea [32]

No. 1 [33]

It has been well said by Dean Church that the spiritual life must be nourished upon ideas not merely kindled by the emotions. When we feel dead and indifferent we are not intended to work ourselves up to a condition of greater fervour; what we want is a new idea of the spiritual life which will act upon that life as does a meal upon a sinking frame. We are to be transformed by the renewing of our minds, and with the renewed vigour given by new thoughts of God we are enabled once more for the spiritual activities of prayer, praise, and godly endeavour. In our Sunday talks we seek for the nutriment of new ideas, and we look for them in one or another of the Gospels, as these afford the most abundant supply of that of which we are in search. Our time is so short that we do not attempt a critical study, but just examine a given passage with a view to those sustaining ideas of the divine life which it may offer. But we take each Gospel as it comes, believing that the teaching is consecutive and that we can no more nourish our souls upon texts selected here and there than we can sustain our bodily or our intellectual life upon scraps.

It is told that Mr. Romanes once asked Darwin to advise him

---

[32] *God is My Light*. Latin title of the Psalm 27 used in the Anglican Book of Common Prayer.

[33] Mason, "Sunday Meditations" *The Parents' Review* 19, no. 3 (March 1908): 222-226. The main text of the meditations generally follows that of the original mail-out subscription collected by Kitching as explained above. These same Sunday talks, with very minor alterations, were eventually published in *The Parent's Review*. I have included the reference to The Parent's Review whenever possible.

as to the best course to take in the pursuit of science. The answer of the elder scientist was, 'meditate.' If meditation be the secret of success in the scientific, how much more must it be so in the spiritual life.

This law of progress was better understood in the earlier Church than it is by ourselves. In the active duties of the Christian life we are apt to lose sight of the importance of meditation. Indeed, this spiritual process is analogous to that of digestion. It is not what we read or what we hear that sustains us, but what we appropriate; what we take home to our minds and ruminate upon,—reading a passage over and over, or dwelling, again and again upon a thought, rejoicing in a 'fresh thought of God' as a thing to be thankful for, a quickening influence to make us alive and active when a palsy of deadness and staleness appears to be creeping over us. We all have a spiritual life to sustain and we all need the periodic nourishment of new, or newly put, thoughts of God. We do not alway sufficiently recognise how our Church has provided for this need in the weekly portion set before us in Collect, Epistle, and Gospel.[34] In these we find, year by year, new thoughts and new teachings unfolding themselves whereby we might well advance to the statures of the perfect man. But our tendency is to grind at one idea until we are worn out with futile efforts and disappointment in ourselves. It is well no to expect too much of ourselves. Not to be too good nor to be happy is the chief thing, but to know, to possess the knowledge of God—'For this is life eternal to know Thee, the only true God, and Jesus Christ whom Thou has sent.'

We are about to begin the study of St. John's Gospel. From this point of view, and it has seemed necessary to explain to those who join us today for the first time the object of our Sunday talks.

---

[34] The Church of England appoints in its Prayer Book a set of 'propers', i.e. a short prayer, called a "collect", followed by an epistle and a gospel lesson for each Sunday of the Liturgical Church Year.

This last of the Gospels is the final revelation of Christ, the last word, so to speak, which comes to us from one who knew; for insight, comprehension, is the privilege of love, and none of the Twelve was so prepared for the fullest inspirations of the Holy Spirit ('Who' says our Lord 'shall testify of Me') as that disciple whom Jesus loved, and who gave the one most welcome return for love—St. John understood his Master.

In reading this Gospel we all feel that we are drinking at the fountain-head of the knowledge of Christ; and from another point of view, the fourth Gospel is singularly comforting and strengthening to us who live in times of much perplexity. The Church has passed through the days when first St. Peter, and later, St. Paul had the teaching to offer specially suited to her needs. Perhaps for the present distress S. John the Divine is the appointed minister. This may be partly due to the fact that the age in which the last Gospel was written was an age of perplexed thought and anxious questionings not unlike our own. S. John is supposed to have written after the fall of Jerusalem, at the close of the first century, when the writer was a very aged man, able to bring from his treasury things new and old. In all probability the Gospel was written at Ephesus and was immediately called for by the state of things in the Christian church generally, but especially in that great sea-port town of Asia Minor, a centre of various life, intellectual an commercial. 'I am of Philo,' 'I am of Plato,' 'I am of Moses,' 'I am of Christ,' men would say, each believing that he held the whole truth; and earnest souls would vex themselves about the difference between Christian and Platonic teaching, that, as they do to-day, about the disparities between the revelation of Scripture and that other revelation of Science which no man is yet able to reconcile.

The aged apostle saw the world about him troubled with many unanswerable questions. Then, as now, many of the best and noblest were not greatly concerned about personal success or failure, but chafed against such problems as—the whence and

whither of men— the meaning of suffering—the mystery of pain—
the purpose of life— the limit of responsibility—the origin of all
things. Some of us to-day see in one divine Person the solution of
every problem; some as in Natural Law in the Spiritual World,[35]
try to make science and religion accord; and confess in the end
that they have failed. Perhaps that we may learn to have the grace
to wait, knowing that God is bringing up the world, and content
meanwhile to believe in what appear to be contrary truths.

But now and then a prophet of God is raised up able to tell us
all things, and such an one is S. John. He did and could reconcile
the difficulties of the early Christian, for the time was come and he
was the man. He was enabled to reveal the mystery of that 'Word'
which was baffling the thought of men. Though the conflict rages
now between science and religion, as then between philosophy
and religion, we also find in the fourth Gospel leaves of the Tree of
Life for the healing of the nations.

'In the beginning was the Word, and the Word was with God
and the Word was God.' Here we have, in a single wonderful
sentence, deliverance from harassing perplexities of the intellect, a
satisfaction for the inmost cravings of the heart. In these days,
when Evolution has changed the basis of human thought, when if
we trace ourselves back to the beginning, we find our origin in
some low form of life, when, if we look forward to the end, we find
if we have lost our first faith, no place for angel or spirit or any
such thing, what a rest of soul it is to know that 'in the beginning
was the Word and The Word was God.' With this knowledge we
can face the beginning and the end. Our painful curiosity about
our origin and our end is not satisfied, but our thoughts are
diverted, and we find rest in the divine Person with whom is all
knowledge.

How satisfying to the hungering heart of man, again, is The

[35] Henry Drummond, *Natural Law in The Spiritual World* (Philadelphia: Henry
Altemus, 1892).

Word. Every Human heart craves for perfect intimacy, comprehension, love, allowance, praise and blame that is just understanding of faults and failures, and of those aspirations which are our true measure. In the Word which is God we find all these. The barrier of flesh are nothing to the Word which is 'quick and powerful as a two-edged sword,' who penetrates our being to comfort, teach, and guide, 'Who knows as we are, yet loves us better than He knows,'[36] for the Word is God, and 'all things are naked and open to the eyes of Him with whom we have to do' (Heb. 4.13). The Word who is God, is our one intimate Friend, our unfailing Companion, and, if the beginning is a 'sunless gulf of doubt' to you, He was there and all is well.

'His name is called the Word of God,' we are told (Rev. 9, 11-16) in almost the closing scene of the Bible, and there we have the vision of the Word in His majesty, and worship before the divine Person. 'The Word was with God.' It is not good for man to be alone, and a lonely, isolated God is remote from the sympathises of men; but, ever, 'the Word was with God,' The perfect love of the divine Son and of the divine Father was there through all eternity.

It would appear as if a different name of Christ, that is, a different aspect of His divine personality were to be presented to men at different states in the history of thought. In earlier days the habit was to speak of Christ as 'the way', for men were looking for a way, In S. John's time men of different schools of though were thinking of the Logos, and striving to reconcile difficulties; in this name, the Word, was the reconciliation they sought. Possibly the new name that will interpret Christ to men, and reconcile, once for science and religion, is 'the life', when God shall have raise up a man to give us this revelation.

(From notes taken by a Student)

---

[36] John Keble, *Christian Year.* 24th Sunday after Trinity.

SCALE HOW 'MEDITATIONS'

Dominus Illumination Mea

No. 2[37]

S. John's Gospel begins with a Prologue (v.1-18) in which the main purpose of the book is set forth in detail, and we shall find each of the indications in the Prologue worked out fully in the Gospel. Taking the 'Word' as the keynote, the object of the Gospel is to reveal this 'Word' in the searching, teaching, inspiring, condemning, forgiving, restoring, vivifying aspects of the Character of our Lord Jesus Christ which the 'Word' includes.

If we read the Gospel, feeling that we have the key in the first verse, we shall see far more deeply into meaning of it than if we read it more at random, though perhaps in a no less devout spirit. The 'Word' contains the solution of all mys teries, comforts all sorrows, cures all diseases, and, above all, gives life. We have (v.2) a confirmation of the statement in verse 1, and the repetition, on account of its rare use, is very impressive. Again (v.3, R.V)[38], we go back to the beginning of all things. 'Without Him was not anything made that hath been made.' 'Hath been' takes in all time. No true picture, poem, invention or discovery 'hath been' made for the use of man but by the 'Word.'

---

[37] Mason, "Sunday Meditations" *The Parents' Review* 19, no. 3 (March 1908): 226-229.

[38] Mason quotes from the Revised Version, a late 19th-century British revision of the King James Version.

All things done perfectly are the result of two persons—the origin and the agent. But, if 'all things' have been made by Him, whence come evil, sin, misery, sickness, death? Many thoughtful people consider that evil is absence of good, that, as the absence of life in the animal and vegetable world means death, and death putrefaction and mortification, so in the spiritual world absence of life means loathsome things of the spirit, hatred, malice, and all uncharitableness. Even acknowledging this as true, we do not find the answer complete. We are born with possibilities good and evil, but the testimony of the 'Word,' and our own experience of sudden suggestions of evil, and then of overflowings of ungodliness, should bring conviction of the access to our spirits of an evil spirit. There is a feeling abroad to-day that there is no external evil personality; that man's good and evil exists in himself. Let us beware of 'spiritual wickedness in high places.' Our conception of Satan is largely Milton's. We have little or no information as to the origin of evil. But to this problem also the answer is 'In the beginning was the 'Word.' Our rightful curiosity is not satisfied, but our fears are appeased and we have, if not the light of knowledge, the rest of perfect confidence.

Again (v.4), we come to another of those problems for which no solution has yet been found—the origin of life. We can chemically analyse protoplasm and recombine the elements, but the result is not life. Seeing there are so many things we cannot know our need for humility is great.

'I know not the way I am going,
But well do I know my Guide.'[39]

---

[39] Hymn from *Spiritual Songs*: VIII.—ISAIAH XLII. 16.

I KNOW not the way I am going,
But well do I know my Guide;
With a child-like trust I give my hand
To the mighty Friend by my side.

The only thing that I say to Him

We do not know the meaning of life or death, but we may learn to know Him in whom are all things.

Light and life are associated; where there is life there is light—the light of the mind, clear undoubting intelligence; the light of the heart, confidence and peace. Light and life arise from the personal presence of our Lord and are not the inheritance of any *denomination*. By this Light we see our Brother, and coming into contact with earnest seekers after truth, who do not speak out shibboleths, we shall not judge them, but think rather 'Lord is it I' who offend?

The 'darkness apprehendeth it not' (v.5). These words are as true in our day of professing Christianity as when they were first spoken. Nothing is more curious than the total failure of the outsider to understand the aims and motives of the Christian life.

We recollect the beautiful history in the earlier Gospels of a birth previous to that of our Lord. Here we find its inner meaning. A man was born with a purpose—'sent from God' to bear witness of the Light (v.8). May we not believe that we too are born with a purpose, and that the purpose is the same? We also are sent from God to bear witness of the light. How can we bear witness? By shining. We must shine, not by efforts to shine, but by keeping in the Light, shining as a planet shines by the light of the sun, thus witnessing to the existence of the sun to a world which has turned away, and so the source of light is invisible. S. John the Baptist proclaimed (v. 8) that he was not shining by his own power, for he said, 'I am not the Christ,' 'I am the voice of one crying in the wilderness.' The Revised Version (v. 9) has 'the Light that lighteth every man *as he* cometh into the world.'

'The thoughts of God are wider

As He takes it, is, "Hold it fast,
Suffer me not to lose my way,
And bring me home at last."

> than the measures of man's mind,
> And the heart of the Eternal
> is most wonderfully kind.'

We think of the heathen as sunken in wickedness, and yet, in spite of unspeakable crime and darkness, we find among savages virtues that put us to shame. It is said that religion is a matter of climate, race, custom, and that the various peoples are best left to their own religions. These peoples shine, so far as they have any virtue, in 'few, faint and feeble' glimmerings of that 'Light which lighteth every man,' but it is the part of Christians to help them to stand in the fuller light of the knowledge of Christ.

There is another question which is the cause of inquietude. Many lead upright, self-denying, beautiful lives, who yet refuse to acknowledge Christ. These also have the 'Light which lighteth every man,' and they dimly see the way, but refuse to raise their eyes to the source of the light.

We know the story of the thirty years in Palestine, 'over whose acres walked those blessed feet,'[40] how 'he came to His own,' the Jews—the people whom God had been educating for thousands of years—and they received Him not. The Jews possess, above other peoples, two virtues, which our gracious Queen, with her usual insight, recognised when, for the walls of the Albert Memorial Chapel she chose Jacob with his piety and family affection to represent two virtues which she saw in her beloved Consort.

But (v.14) to those who received Him, to them gave He power to *become* the children of God. '*Become*' implies progression, eternal progression we may believe towards that goal which our Master has set before us as children of God—'Be ye perfect, as your Father which is in Heaven is perfect.' We realize some of the joy of the eternity before us when we regard it as an opportunity for endless progress in love, in power, intelligence, in successful

---

[40] Shakespeare, *King Henry the IV*, Part I: Act 1, Scene 1.

endeavour, in glorious activities, in the knowledge of our God and Father, we wonder how the universe itself can afford scope for the full life of such beings as it lies before us to 'become' as children of God.

And what is the first step in this 'becoming?'—That we receive,' or believe, in the 'Word.' The two terms appear to be synonymous: to 'receive' is to 'believe in', and to 'believe in' is to receive. We use 'accept' in a somewhat similar sense when a woman accepts her future husband. Such reception of our Lord is and act of recognition, and to know another we must think about, consider, ponder that other.

There was once a man suffering the extreme of bodily anguish, torn by remorse for the past and the terrors of the judgment to come, who was so arrested by the personality of another that he forgot himself and pondered upon that other for three hours. Then he was able to say 'Lord.' The thief on the cross is a parable for us. If we should receive and believe on our Lord, even so must we ponder upon Him to the forgetting of ourselves, even of our sins and shortcomings.

(From notes taken down by a student)

———————

Note.—there will be no 'meditations' for 6th as Miss Mason is ill, the next will arrive, all being well, for Sunday, 13th inst.

SCALE HOW 'MEDITATIONS'
Dominus Illuminatio Mea.

No. 3

[Sunday,] February 13th, 1898.

S. John's Gospel: the Prologue, verses 12-18[41]
(v. 12) To believe in His Name, —'Is given to Faith, affectionate and free, Not wrought by force of self-confounding thought.'[42]

(v.13) A man cannot work himself into belief from any motives of what has well been called 'eternal selfishness'—'not for the sake of gaining Heaven nor of escaping Hell'—not by the will of the flesh is the faith born which recognizes the Word, neither by the will of man—no intellectual effort, no self-confounding thought, will

---

[41] Mason, *The Parents' Review* 17, no. 9 (September 1906): 709-713.

[42] Hartley Coleridge, Poems II, "*The Bible*" (London: Edward Moxon, 1851): 339.

> How very good is God! that he hath taught
> To every Christian that can hear and see
> Both what he is and what he ought to be,
> And how and why the saints of old have fought.
> Whate'er of truth the antique sages sought,
> And could but guess of his benign decree,
> Is given to Faith affectionate and free,
> Not wrung by force of self-confounding thought.
>
> How many generations had gone by
> 'Twixt suffering Job and boding Malachi!
> 'Twixt Malachi and Paul—how mute a pause!
> Is the book finish'd? May not God once more
> Send forth a prophet to proclaim his laws
> In holy words not framed by human lore?

discover the Word to us— but by the will of God we believe. Let us not suppose that God wills, chooses, that some of us should receive the power to become the sons of God and others should never have this power. Is it not rather that our will must embrace the will of God, must accept the ineffable mystery, adore the grace, be so united with the will of God that no perplexity baffles our understanding, because we do not seek[43] to understand? Then to Faith, affectionate and free, the vision of the Son of God is possible, and, with the vision, comes the power to become more and more, eternally, the child of God.

(v. 14) 'The Word became flesh.' In these four words we have summed up the story before which myriads of Christian souls have bowed in tender reverence—the story of the Birth in Bethlehem. It would seem as if, in all ages and in all countries, there had been in human hearts a desire, so universal as to be prophetic of its own fulfilment,—the desire that 'the gods' would 'come down to us in the likeness of men.'[44] Our hearts are wiser than our heads; the intellect of man says, 'this thing is impossible;' the heart insists that this is the only satisfaction for its wistful desires, that there must be a Man, Who fulfils all that is possible to man, Who is God, and Who links us with God. 'And dwelt among us,' not visited us as the wind, we know not whence or whither, but went in and out among us with human ways like our ways and needs like our needs and tendernesses like our tendernesses, so that we could rivet our eyes upon Him and see and be satisfied. 'And we beheld His glory,' says S. John, not his,—

'To overlook the glory close and near;'[45]

---

[43] Changed to "We do not expect to understand" in 1906 republication.

[*] Acts 14:11.

[45] Richard Monckton Milnes "The Burden of Egypt," *Palm Leaves* (London: Edward Moxon, 1844) 156.

He beheld with the fixed gaze of love and discipleship, and he knew that that which he beheld of lowly living and service and suffering was 'glory.' Perhaps this is one of the secrets of life—to know 'glory' when we see it. Moses prayed, 'I beseech Thee show me Thy glory,' and the answer was, 'I will make all My goodness pass before thee,' and for three and thirty years all the goodness of God, which is His glory, passed up and down in the eyes of men.

'I ever taught,' He says, 'where all the Jews come together.' The luxury of seclusion was not for Him. A life never out of sight was a life always divine; but only the few disciples 'beheld.' The rest of the world judged Him according to its own measure and called Him names which it pains us to repeat. His 'glory' is still in the world, not in the full measure in which S. John beheld it, but a little here and a little there wherever any humble soul seeks to walk in the light and to go about doing good. May we behold His 'glory' wherever it is, and cast from our eyes all bandages of pride and prejudice which could blind us to a single ray of the light that comes from Him.

'Full of grace and truth'; here are the tests by which we shall know His glory wherever it shines. 'Grace' is hard to define; 'the touch of God' an old writer calls it, and perhaps we can go no further; but our every-day words 'graceful' and 'gracious' help us. The quite fit action or word is, we say, 'graceful,' and we can say no more. We mean that it is the very word which should have been spoken, said just at the right time, just in the right way, neither more nor less than was fitting, or the very act that should have been done. 'Gracious' implies more; the word or the act is not only beautifully fit in itself, but is kind and cordial and fit towards us who receive it. It comes to us with a smiling benediction. The baby who stretches out a hand to one does the little act with a strange graciousness. Our gracious Queen is 'gracious' when she sits beside the beds of her sick soldiers; the act is so fit and so perfect in itself and towards them. Now and then *we* may say graceful things, and do gracious things; but with what a sense of infinite goodness comes before us that Life which was full of grace, which never, no not for an instant, entertained an ungracious thought. And these conceptions of 'graceful' and 'gracious' touch only the fringe of the garment of grace. It was well for S. John to behold this 'glory.' May our eyes also be unveiled!

'And truth'—At the first glance we do not find ourselves quail[46] before this standard of measurement as before the other. We may not be gracious or graceful, we say, but at any rate we are honest. Are we? What of the idle talk with which we entertain each other? Does nothing pass our lips but that which is our sincere, carefully thought-out conviction? Do we never express regard or consideration or approval or disapproval but in the exact measure in which we feel it? We need not go on with such questions as these: we are convicted before the first, and feel that absolute truth is impossible to us. But this man, Whose 'glory' S. John beheld, walked about in the world with a lamp of truth, as it were, whose ray flashed straight into the heart of every subject he spoke upon, every person He looked upon; and new things, strange things, an inverted order of things, came to light,—the last became first and the first became last. May He illuminate us with his truth that we may see His 'glory' in the things which are least, and not be dazzled by the sham glory of the things which the world calls great.

(v. 15) We return to the witness of S. John Baptist. 'He is become before me,' the Baptist says, 'for He was before me.' Probably we have here the secret of all witness for Christ. It appears so simple that we are inclined to say, 'Of course.' 'Of course' Christ was before the Baptist, and 'of course' Christ is before us in the sense of the one with the greater claims. Surely of this there can be no question. Well for us if we can say this in spirit and in truth, for the essence of all idolatry lies in this—the preferring of 'I, myself' to any other—to the Christ of God. This

---

[46] To shrink back with fear; cower.

besetment is so subtle that we can hardly be aware of it. It takes the guise of penitence, anxiety, humility, of the feelings we call our best and holiest. But self-occupation, whether in the form of self-depreciation or self-exaltation, is giving self the place of preference which is due to Another. It is less easy, than it seems, to arrive at the standpoint of the Baptist and to recognise that in all things Christ is before us, is of more consequence than we are, is to be considered and thought upon first in all our troubles and perplexities. This is not born of the flesh; it is of God.

(v. 16) but the sense of spiritual effort need not depress us. The fullness which S. John beheld and proceeds to set before us, in the Gospel, is for us all: we all receive of it and 'grace for grace.' 'The phrase means a continual recurrence of kindnesses.'[47] This is a phrase to be thankful for. We are all aware of the continual kindnesses of God. Every day brings some surprising delicacy of kindness that touches us, and yet we do not boldly say to ourselves—'This is a special kindness shown to me by God; This comes out of the fullness of the grace and graciousness of Jesus Christ.' If he is so wonderfully kind in the small things of every-day life, he will not be less kind in the greater things. He Himself will enable us to put Him in that first place in our thoughts which belongs to Him and to leave off troubling about ourselves. This is due to us of His grace.

(v. 17) 'The law was given by Moses.' I suppose most of us grow up under the discipline of the law. 'I must try and leave some fault behind while I am young. I am trying very hard to do so, but I find it very difficult. I think of Life's Ladder; every fault I conquer I get one step higher, do I not?' I quote from the letter of a little girl. We all go through it. We all know what it is to toil up this ladder of perfection and, when we think we have gained a round or two, to find we have slipped back to the old place or lower; but, 'grace and truth came by Jesus Christ.' Grace, continual kindness, help, and

---

* "Rythmic Translation" *of The Imitation of Christ.*

comfort. Truth, revelation, insight, the power to see Him as He is and, in the strength of love, to rise into that holiness which is not individual perfection, though that also comes of it. But the power to put Him first.

(v. 18) This is how we may know God and see Him Who is invisible. The Son hath declared Him, hath revealed to us a mystery, inconceivable to the heart of man, the Humility of our God.

It would seem to us almost a pity to touch upon in advance, and in a cursory way, many thoughts that are worked out in detail as the Gospel goes on, but this is S. John's method. He begins with a prologue which arrests our attention, stirs our heart, touches the deepest things of our life, puts us, in fact, into that attitude of mind which would enable us to perceive, as he goes on to unveil the Word, a little now and a little again as we are able to bear it.

SCALE HOW 'MEDITATIONS'

Dominus Illuminatio Mea

No. 4
February 20th, 1898

(S. John 1, 18-29)
THE WITNESSS OF THE BAPTIST[48]

We read in the other Gospels of the religious revival which the preaching of the Baptist had brought about. It does not belong to the purpose of the writer of the Fourth Gospel to tell us of the multitudes who came to hear the Preacher in the wilderness; but it was evident to all men that an important religious movement was going on and the Church at Jerusalem could not ignore it. Besides, they also were looking for some great One and—might not this be He? He appeared amongst them at any rate with the credentials of a prophet which had ever been found in a message.

(v. 19) This man had plainly a message, and his hermit life and his hermit dress, keeping up the tradition of the prophets added a certain authority to his message; so the rulers of the Jews sent a deputation to ask the Baptist who he was. He might even be the Christ Himself, for, though prophesy is so luminous in the light of its fulfilment, the Jews do not appear to have looked for prophet, king, priest, and sacrificial victim, in One.

(v. 20) John confessed and denied not. He said 'I am not the Christ.' We can conceive that even he might have been misled by

---

[48] Mason, *The Parents' Review 17*, no. 9 (September 1906): 713-716.

his success as a preacher into an awed questioning with himself as to whether he were indeed the coming One. But the preacher in the wilderness escaped this danger because his thoughts were not concerned with himself.

(v. 21) His questioners seemed determined to find in him the fulfilment of prophecy, and they were right and John was wrong. 'Art thou Elijah?'[49] they say, looking for the fulfilment of the prediction in Malachi. And he said, 'I am not.' But our Lord says of him 'And if ye will receive it, this is Elijah which was for to come.'[50] * Teachers sent from God hardly recognise the significance of their work; much less that they themselves have been thought of from of old in the counsels of God. One more question—'Art thou the Prophet?'—the Prophet like unto himself, whose coming was foretold by Moses,[51]** who was to be, as he, a leader and commander of the people. 'No,' was the simple answer.

(v. 22) The questioners are baffled and begin to be displeased. If the Baptist has indeed no divine sanction, what right has he to carry away people with his authoritative preaching? What account has he to give of himself?

(v. 23) John replies by a figure, familiar to the prophets, taken from the progress of an Eastern Monarch. To this day it is the same. The King is preceded by his messengers who run before him hot-foot crying—'Make ready the way, make ready the way,' and every labourer who hears is bound to leave his work in the fields and hasten to mend the rusts or even to lay miles of road, where none existed, that the King may have a smooth progress. The Baptist has declared his mission; he is not the Christ, but his coming is a certain proclamation of the near approach of Him who was the expectation of the Jews.

---

* Malachi 4:5.

** S. Matthew 9:14.

*** Deut. 18:18.

(v. 25) They understand well enough this reference to the prophecy of Isaiah,[52] but they are captious; they are not ready to receive that which they hear; and so they challenge John's right to baptise if he has no authority to make disciples.

(v. 26) It might be that at that moment the eye of the speaker alighted upon Him whom he had just proclaimed as King. 'I baptise with water,' he says, 'to repentance, that the people may be ready; but, in the midst of you, among you at this moment, all unaware to you while you question me, standeth that very One, the King, for whom I am not worthy to do the office of the humblest slave.

We long to know the rest, whether conviction came to this deputation of the Jews and what answer they took to those that sent them. But these are not important matters. Most important for us, parents and teachers, helpers and guides in any way to those about us, it is to study this example of a man sent from God to bear witness of the Light. To all of us who get a following of disciples, if it be only the little ones about our knee, are put these very questions to which the Baptist was able to give faithful answers. We, who teach and train, can hardly do better than to take S. John the Baptist as our patron saint, and prepare ourselves by his example, with unconscious answers to the questions which are unconsciously put to us. Whenever we allow our little following to suppose that our opinions are final, our authority absolute and self-sustained, our teaching right an other teaching wrong; whenever we try to hem them in by the narrow thoughts of the school, the sect, the family, are we not failing from the faithfulness of the Baptist? Are we indeed giving his simple and emphatic denial, 'I am not the Christ?' Well for us if our Master should say to each of us, as to the Baptist, 'Friend, go up higher,' (This is Elijah which was for to come); and, when we say in our humility—'we are no heaven-sent teachers with a special

---

* Isaiah 40: 3

message from God,' He should say of us that we too are, in our small way, prophets and teachers sent forth by Him to bear witness of the Light.

Once more the Baptist sets us an example. He does not choose to be anybody; He empties himself, he has no personal claims, he is 'a voice,' a voice whose office it is to herald the approach, proclaim the nearness, of our King. In a sense each of us is a voice we all seek expression; the more modes of expression we find, the fuller and richer is our life. Expression is to us life; suppression, death. But not all voices utter the same name. Does a great artist paint a picture and behind and through the marvellous technique, does his inspiring idea speak to our souls? If so, the artist utters another Name than his own. But are we content to admire the picture for itself and in itself? Does it fail to reach out of itself towards any of those thoughts by which men live, though it be in the broad sweep of a sky, the seal upon a countenance? In such a picture the artist utters a name, but it is his own. It is not only the great works of great people that express a name. We all remember the vivid scene in that carpenter's shop where Adam and Seth Bede each produce a door. Seth, though he had great spiritual searchings of heart, made a door which expressed his own name, a poor, incomplete, thing, the scoff of the workshop. Adam, though he would not have called himself religious, made a door fit and perfect; which expressed the highest Name.[53] It is well to remember that, not only in our words but in our works and ways, we must needs express always a name, that name which is above everything to us, and which must needs be either our own poor name or the name of Him who stands amongst us in our midst and whose shoe's latchet we are not worthy to unloose.

In one more respect we, as teachers, shall do well to consider the example of the Baptist. He had only one concern,—'to prepare the way of the Lord,'—and we may lay it to heart that our teaching

---

[53] George Eliot - *Adam Bede*, Chapter I "The Worskshop."

is effective only as it works towards this end. 'There is only one thing worth living for—'to be of use'—has been well said, and we may believe that every act of service, whether for the health, the virtue, or the happiness of the community, is a preparation of the way.

(v. 29) How 'deed enlarges scope!'[54] On the morrow, and again on the next morrow, come new opportunities for the Baptist to bear witness for Christ, and he seizes each opportunity. This witness of his is recognised by his Master. 'Ye have sent unto John, and he hath born witness of the Truth,' says our Lord;[55] and Christ is no man's debtor. He, in turn, bears witness of John: 'Among them that are born of women there hath not arisen a greater,[56*] He says, who knows all things from the beginning. So we find it to-day. Every poor little word of witness of ours is so abundantly magnified and made fruitful by the Word Himself that we are amazed. If our witness persistently fails, we had better examine ourselves. There is one common source of failure, what the prophet describes as 'bowing down to our own nets.'[57] Perhaps this is the unsuspected defect in most of the teaching that fails in its witness.[58]

---

[54] George MacDonald, *The Disciple* (London: Strahan and Co, 1867) 40.

<blockquote>
'What is his will? –that I may go
And do it now, in hope
That light will rise and spread and flow
As deed enlarges scope.
</blockquote>

* S. John 5:33 (R.V.)

** S. Luke 7:28.

[57] Habakkuk 1:16 'Therefore he sacrifices to his net and makes offerings to his dragnet; for by them he lives in luxury, and his food is rich.'

[58] Good teaching prepares the way for giving witness to the light, Self-centered teaching fails in its witness to the Name therefore it is a failure.

SCALE HOW 'MEDITATIONS'
Dominus Illuminatio Mea

No. 5 [59]

S. John 1:29-34 [60]

(v. 29) How graphic the picture is. We see 'the mild Son of Man'[61] drawing near with that gracious dignity which we know must have been His; as He approaches a word of amazing insight is given to the Baptist. The tender image of 'the Lamb of God' is so dear and so familiar to us that we can hardly realize that it came to the Baptist as a sudden flash illuminating the whole history of the Jews since their deliverance from Egypt and opening up the meaning of every Paschal Feast,—and this, of a Man, standing in their midst! It must have been to the disciples of the Baptist a very shock of revelation:—'In this man, of countenance so benign, of aspect so meek and lowly, behold the interpretation of all the sacrificial rites which have become to you a religion in themselves. Behold in this Man the great deliverance: it is He that taketh away the sin of the world!'

How could they receive so great a gospel for which they were so little prepared? Can we receive it? Do we receive it when we are overwhelmed with the thought of our own unworthiness, of the unspeakable wickedness in the world? But John, for this moment at any rate, entered into the larger hope. Looking a fellow-Man in the face, unfettered by the limitations of sense and circumstance, he could say 'which taketh away the sin'—not of the Jews, but—'the sin of the world.' Only as we have this faith, have we

---

[59] Themes: Vocation; Sacramental essence of nature; The Holy Spirit.

[60] Mason, *The Parents' Review* 17, no. 9 (September 1906): 716-719. Also, re-published in *The Parents' Review* 19, no. 5 (May 1908): 382-385.

[61] John Keble, "Quinquagesima Sunday" *The Christian Year.*

faith enough to go on with; can we believe—of the sins which make us mourn, of the faults which vex us in those dear to us, of the depths of wickedness which are without us on every side, —that He taketh away all this sin; taketh with a constant, steady, unceasing action of taking until in the end He hath taken all away, and there shall be no more sin.

(v. 30) Again while all eyes are turned upon the approaching Presence, John takes occasion to repeat his saying about the precedence of Christ; no mere social precedence such as we yield to those above us in rank, but, as we have it in the marginal reading. 'First in regard of me,' the greatest concern of all his concerns, the subject of his continual thoughts, the object of all his desires. Nor was the Baptist satisfied withal that he had attained; we read elsewhere this deep law of the Christian life as formulated by him—'He must increase, but I must decrease.'

(v. 31) 'And I knew Him not.' The two related families may not have met, or, in his kinsman, John may not have recognised the Christ. But the stir of His coming was in the air and we may believe that much of John's wilderness life was spent in meditation upon the character and work of the coming Messiah—the more intent and passionate because he knew that he himself was the forerunner, that, indeed, his baptism with water should be as it were a condition of the manifestation of Christ.

'For this cause:'—How well for John to know his life sanctified by a great purpose which was not of his choosing but was his vocation, calling. And how rich is our life, too, when we perceive that there is no calling among men too lowly to have for its purpose the manifestation of Christ. Pleasant ways and kindly words and simple duty-doing, in these things of every-day life Christ is manifested.

(v. 32). 'And John bare witness saying,'—This introduction seems to point to a testimony borne on still another occasion.

There is no direct account given in the Gospel of S. John of Our Lord's baptism, only this indirect reference made by the Baptist. To him, as to each of us, the revelation of Christ came by the Holy Spirit; 'he beheld the Spirit descending as a dove out of heaven and it abode upon Him.' Most of us have observed how the everyday sights of the natural world have been hallowed, whether by association with our Lord, or, by His use of them to convey deeper truths. The lambs upon the hillside, the reeds in our lakes, the shepherd and his flock, the grass, the cornfield, the wind, the face of the sky, the sea and the fishing boats and the fisher folk, and many other sweet natural associations, are as bonds of sympathetic thought between us and our Lord. But perhaps we fail to realize that those things which He observes with His eyes and hallows by naming with His lips, are but types of the rest chosen to point to us the fact that nature teems with teaching of the things of God, that every leaf on every tree is inscribed with the divine Name, that the myriad sounds of summer are articulate voices, that all nature is symbolic, or as has been better said, is sacramental. Realizing the close correspondence and interdependence between things natural and things spiritual, that God nowhere leaves Himself without a witness, and that every beauteous form and sweet sound is charged with teaching for us, had we eyes to see and ears to hear, we shall better understand any single emblem brought before us than if we suppose it to bee chosen arbitrarily and taken away from its connection with the natural world.

The Church of Christ has always loved this emblem of a dove, this embodiment which the Holy Spirit assumed when He descended upon Christ and abode with Him. The dove, 'sweet messenger of rest,' moving upon the face of the waters, was a pledge of restoration; its return to the Ark typified the homing instinct of men; tenderness and peace, confidence and comfort, constancy an sweetness abiding love, unfailing gentleness, quiet ways, these are among the notions which men by nature associate with the dove, and which through his image we learn to associate with the 'Gracious Spirit, heavenly Dove.'[62] It is worth while to consider the meanings that our great nature-poet finds in the dove—though they have no obvious reference to the event of the Baptism.

> 'I heard a Stock-dove sing or say
> his homely tale, this very day:...
> He sang of love, with quiet blending,
> Slow to begin, and never ending;
> Of serious faith, and inward glee;
> That was the Son—the Song for me!'[63]

It is solacing to the heart of Christendom to know that our blessed Lord was not without the comfort of this 'mutual love,' 'serious faith,' 'inward glee,' that the joy of the Lord was with Him even while He dwelt among us, a man of sorrows. What a thought of joy at the baptismal font, of consolation throughout life amid the tossing of the waves of this troublesome world, is this of the divine Spirit coming to us, also, in the likeness of a dove. It was by the dove which rested upon Him that John was taught to know his Lord; and, wherever Christ is, the Divine Spirit will brood in gentleness and tenderness, in quietness and confidence, and in unspeakable 'inward glee;' for, 'He baptiseth with the Holy Spirit.'

(v. 34) 'He shall testify of Me' Says our Lord of the Divine Spirit. So it was with John. With the coming of the Spirit he reached the summit of the mount of vision. He was at his greatest; for, according to our faith and insight, is our power for action and

---

[62] Hymn:

> Come, Gracious Spirit, heavenly Dove,
> with light and comfort from above;
> be thou our guardian, thou our guide
> o'er every thought and step preside.

[63] William Wordsworth, "O Nightingale, Thou Surely Art." *Poems of Wordsworth*. Ed. Matthew Arnold (London: Macmillan & Co, 1898): 141.

influence, 'Great is the mystery of godliness, God manifest in the flesh':—the Baptist sees it all,—'this is the Son of God,' of the essence of the Father, very God of very God.[64] To know this of a Man standing in the midst of other men was indeed triumphant faith. As our Lord said after to S. Peter, when he too saw the veil lifted, 'flesh and blood hath not revealed this unto thee, but my Father which is in heaven.' Only so can any of us know the Christ. 'Lord increase our faith.'

---

[64] This is the language of the Creed.

SCALE HOW 'MEDITATIONS'
Dominus Illuminatio Mea

No. 6[65]
March 6th, 1898

THE CALL OF THE FIRST DISCIPLES[66]
(S. John 1:35-43)

(v. 35) Once more we have the testimony of the Baptist, but his is no longer the figure of central interest. He was standing at the baptistry of his, that pool of Jordan, at Bethany or Bethabara; and with him stood two of his disciples after a manner no longer understood in the western world. A man's disciples to-day read his books or attend his lectures, but in the East and in the academic groves of Athens disciples followed their master up and down to gather stray words of wisdom from his lips.

(v. 36) 'And he looked upon Jesus as He walked.' We have all experienced at some time and in a measure the feeling implied in this phrase. When Nansen[67] stood, small to behold among his thousands of auditors, and told how he had faced unaided and alone the great forces of nature, one looked at him with amazement that so much vitality, energy and resource could be contained within the small compass of a single man. Those who

---

[65] Mason, *The Parents' Review* 19, no. 5 (May 1908): 385-389.

[66] Some key themes of this meditation are: New wine of life; vocation; disciples; the searching question of a great teacher; nothing is so catching as conviction; We see in this story the limit of what we can do for one another; The less religiosity in our language, the more we are able to speak simply; Our teaching will command attention; If we are persons whose observations are worth heeding; *rapport;* spirit with spirit, person with person.

[67] Fridtjof Nansen, artic explorer.

looked upon Florence Nightingale, Tennyson, Browning, Darwin, must have been overtaken now and then by similar amazement. The Baptist looked at the (apparently retreating) figure of the Son of Man, overwhelmed by the sense of all which that single human form represented; out of the fullness of his heart an utterance came; he has said the same words before, and we may believe that he repeats them because to him they express the most of that which Christ is—'Behold the Lamb of God.' They enunciate a new principle of life, dimly hinted at indeed by prophets, practised, more or less, by many a loving soul, but never before brought out in relief as the truth by which men live. The principle of sacrifice was old and was common to all the world. The principle of voluntary self-sacrifice for the behoof of others was new; and, just as we say a man is generous, or witty, or patriotic, putting our finger upon his characteristic, the master-thought of all this thinking, so the Baptist pointed to Christ as the Lamb of God,—always in the act of out pouring His life for the sustenance of His people. 'I, if I be lifted up, will draw all men unto Me,' says our Lord in perhaps the most pregnant of His sayings, that one which more than any other teaches us the meaning of Calvary. Possibly the thought of Christian people has been a good deal obscured as to the meaning of the Atonement which our Lord made. He died for us. Yes: but we are apt in the face of this mystery to lose sight of the constraining force of His life, reaching down and forth towards our lives, and drawing them upward to the place where He is: the place where no man thinks first of himself, but values his life only that he also may lay it down and spend it to the uttermost for his brethren. This is, perhaps, some of the force which the Baptist perceived in 'that continual dying which constrains us'[68]—the Lamb of God.

(v. 37) The two disciples—one of them, we may suppose, the

[68] 'For the love of Christ constrains us; because we thus judge, that if one died for all, then were all dead.' 2 Corinthians 5:14

Evangelist himself, the other Andrew, that gentle saint who was among the inner group of the Twelve chosen to be with our Lord on some special occasion, because, we may believe, they loved much— the two, amazed, like men in a dream, apparently bewildered by the great conceptions brought before them, turned without any words of farewell and left the Baptist and followed Christ.

(v. 38) We are aware of it when we are being followed, and it appears to be with that natural human consciousness that our Lord turns and addresses the two. According to His wont, he addressed to them the searching question of a great teacher, which is, at the same time, the ordinary phrase which any man would use— 'What seek ye?' We should do well to meditate on these words, because they are possibly the direct question that Christ addresses to many of us. He brings us to pause in the midst of a giddy or restless career with some such query—'What are you aiming at? What will be the result of all these efforts? What do you propose to yourself in the end? You cannot believe that a little success, or a little pleasure, or a little wealth, or a little of the friendship and favour of men will satisfy you! What seek ye?'

(v. 39) The two make answer awkwardly enough in their shame-facedness—'Master, where dwellest Thou?' or, as we should say—'Where do you live?' probably before the words were well spoken they chided themselves for their rude clumsiness; and yet they gave the very answer which it behoves us to give when Christ meets us, soul to soul, and demands— 'What seekest thou?' We, too, would do well to answer, question for question— 'Master, where dwellest Thou?' 'We seek the place where Thou art, for there would we also be, for in truth Thou art the end of all the searchings of heart which perplex us.'

Observe the fullness of grace and the sweetness of courtesy with which our Lord replies to what the two doubtless felt to be their rude demand. 'Come and ye shall see,' He says, and they went with Him, and saw where He abode. We wonder where it was. We know of no hospitable roof which covered Him in those early days in Judea. We know that 'the foxes have holes and the birds of the air have nests, but the Son of Man hath not where to lay his head;' But He appears to have had an abode for the time, and the two went with Him, and it was the tenth hour (four o'clock in the afternoon), and 'they abode with Him that day.' The day ended at six o'clock, so they had two hours talk with our Master and theirs. The discovery of the six possible Logia of Christ at Oxyrhynchus[69] has greatly moved the Christian world, but what would it be to us if these two had made notes, not on their hearts only but on some old papyri, of that two hour's discourse in which our Lord gave Himself unsparingly, not only in teaching, but in that virtue of His life which is self-sacrifice for service's sake? But we know nothing. As the sun set they came out from Him, too full we may believe for speech, having drunk of that new wine of life which should henceforth make every petty detail of every day living worth while to them.

(v. 40) 'One of the two was Andrew, Simon Peter's brother.'

(v. 41) 'And he findeth first his own brother Simon, 'Simon the hasty an impetuous, Simon the unstable and the firm, the meek and the proud the most loveably human perhaps of all the Twelve. It was possibly not quite easy for Andrew to give his great news to Simon; we all know that it is not easy to impart confidences to the hasty in speech, rapid in judgment, who will not let us say our say before they come down upon us with objections. But Andrew went to work the shortest and the surest way. He told his tale without preamble. In much and in little it was this—'We have found the Messiah.' A statement so startling from the brother whose greater composure of mind and steadfastness of character had possibly great weight with Simon succeeded anyway in bringing him up

---

[69] Two Lectures on the 'Sayings of Jesus' Recently Discovered at Oxyrhynchus ... By William Sanday, Walter Lock 1897.

suddenly. Had Andrew set out with elaborate attempts to prove that his new teacher was the Messiah, His brother would doubtless have found argument for argument and would not in the end have been convinced. But nothing is so catching as conviction.

(v. 42) Andrew was sure and made no attempt to show why; and Simon was arrested and ready for the next step, which was, that ' he brought him unto Jesus.'

Here follows an example of the intimate personal communication which our Lord holds with every person that comes to Him. We see in this story the limit of what we can do for one another. We can arrest the attention of another; and that, only by the intensity and absoluteness of our own conviction. Perhaps, too, we should do well to imitate Andrews and express our conviction in few strong, plain words. The less religiosity in our language, the more we are able to speak simply and plainly as we do about other things and other people, the more chance there is that we shall be attended to. Then, too, our own character tells. If we are persons whose observations are worth heeding, we may be able to arrest the attention of another, and fix it upon that life which who so contemplates sincerely must needs adore. But that is all we can do. Just as we may introduce a friend to a friend and the introduction may end there or may be followed up into great intimacy and mutual comprehension, so it is with Christ; there can be no intermediary dealings with Him, but close *rapport,* person with person. We should understand all this better if we could leave off thinking that our personality is the visible body which our friends look upon with their eyes. When we realise that we deal with each other, spirit with spirit, person with person, the outer form of us being a mere by-issue, interesting but not vital, then we shall understand that in just the same real, personal, way we must need come face to face with Christ.

(v. 43) 'Jesu looked upon him,' a look of discernment, of

complete recognition, a look that appreciates all the influences of His education and environment— 'thou art Simon the son of John'—a look which recognises in the turbulent, restless nature the latent possibility of perfect repose and strength:—Christ gave him a new name—'thou shalt be called Cephas, Peter, a rock.'

Dominus Illuminatio Mea[70]

No. 7
March 13th, 1898

THE CALL OF PHILIP AND NATHANAEL[71]
(S. John 1:43-51)

We have seen in the call of the first two disciples and of Peter two of our Lord's most winning characteristics—His *accessibility*: He appears to be always at leisure for any who would see Him, always open to demands upon His service. In His words to Peter, again we notice the complete *sympathy* which is the only key to perfect appreciation of character. It is as if the one consciousness were projected into the other and a life-history read at a glance.

(v. 43) As the narrative goes on we have more opportunities of seeing how our Lord deals, not with men, but with each man on the fully recognised basis of his personality. 'On the morrow.' This is the fourth day that the Evangelist describes minutely, day by day. No wonder! We could all write at great length of the first two or three days of our stay in a new country. S. John does something more. He, an aged man, writes of the intense impressions he received upon entering, not a foreign country, but a new life. 'He was minded to go forth into Galilee.' Nothing is

---

[70] Mason, *The Parents' Review* 19, no. 5 (May 1908): 463-468.

[71] Themes: Apparent insurmountable difficulties; doubts; are born of our limitations; fuller scientific knowledge may dispel doubt; the force of conviction; friendship; the best that is possible; 'it is according to our desires, even according to our aspirations, that God deals with us;' accessibility; how our Lord deals, not with men, but with each man; preferable conditions of life for a fine and enduring physical development and for vigorous and untrammelled intellectual force; guileless as a child.

casual or unimportant in the narrative. He was *minded*. This first Galilean circuit was part of the *intention* of His ministry. Had he sought for advice, no doubt it would have run:—'Remain in Judea, for there are the Jews and the Christ is to come as King of the Jews. Go to Jerusalem, for there are the learned and religious among the people; they will give a hearing to a prophet.' But in this journey to Galilee we have the first indication of the fulfilment of the Baptist's witness that Christ came to take away the sins of the world. He was brought up as a Galilean, his apostles were Galileans, much of his ministry was performed in Galilee because, we may believe, Galilee was a connecting link between the Gentile world and the Jews— 'Galilee of the Gentiles'—the province was inhabited by a mixed race planted here by the conquerors when the Jews were carried into Babylon—'the people that walked in darkness saw a great light.'

'He findeth Philip and saith unto him, 'Follow me." That is all; we are not even told that Philip obeyed—that is a matter of course. But how full is the brief narrative. We have another example here of our Lord's prescience and full recognition of the man He is speaking to. We give commands only to those of whose obedience we are assured. Here no preliminaries were necessary. Philip waited for no revelation of himself. He stood as a soldier 'at attention,' waiting the word of command.

(v.44) His preparedness is, in some measure, accounted for by the words which follow—'Now Philip was of Bethsaida, the city of Andrew and Peter.' Perhaps these young men had talked often one with another of that 'expectation of the Jews' which was at hand. The news of the momentous interviews with which his friends had been honoured would find in him an eager and acquiescent listener. Just so did he find it in his heart to believe in the Messiah. In every age of the Church, and not least in our own, there have been saints of God waiting with child like simplicity for the Word; they hear and they follow because their hearts are already prepared for the mandate which shall give order and purpose to their lives.

(v. 45) 'Philip findeth Nathanael.' Observe, no one of these first disciples can keep the new joy of his life to himself. He must find someone else to share his gladness. 'Love and a fire cannot be hid,'[72] and this is true, above all, of the love of Christ. This is no treasure which we can contain without imparting. The secrets will out, perhaps in words to a chosen friend here and there, perhaps it may be our vocation to tell that which we know to many. But if we say no words at all we shall assuredly betray that we have been with Christ by the 'sweetness and light'[73] which the

---

[72] "Violets? What violets?" asked the other, with an unsuccessful effort to appear indifferent. "Those in your room. They scent the house. Love and a fire cannot be hid, neither can violets." Maxwell Gray, *The Reproach of Annesley* (Leipzig: Bernhard Tauchnitz, 1889) 102.

[73] "The pursuit of perfection, then, is the pursuit of sweetness and light. He who works for sweetness and light, works to make reason and the will of God prevail. He who works for machinery, he who works for hatred, works only for confusion. Culture looks beyond machinery, culture hates hatred; culture has one great passion, the passion for sweetness and light. It has one even yet greater! — the passion for making them prevail. It is not satisfied till we all come to a perfect man; it knows that the sweetness and light of the few must be imperfect until the raw and unkindled masses of humanity are touched with sweetness and light. If I have not shrunk from saying that we must work for sweetness and light, so neither have I shrunk from saying that we must have a broad basis, must have sweetness and light for as many as possible."

"The ordinary popular literature is an example of this way of working on the masses. Plenty of people will try to indoctrinate the masses with the set of ideas and judgments constituting the creed of their own profession or party. Our religious and political organizations give an example of this way of working on the masses. I condemn neither way; but culture works differently. It does not try to teach down to the level of inferior classes; it does not try to win them for this or that sect of its own, with ready-made judgments and watchwords. It seeks to do away with classes; to make the best that has been thought and known in the world current everywhere; to make all men live in an atmosphere of sweetness and light, where they may use ideas, as it uses them itself, freely,— nourished and not bound by them. This is the social idea; and the men of culture are the true apostles of equality. The great men of culture are those who have had a

countenance of our Lord has shed upon us. Then follows Philip's confession of Faith, one more *credo*. We do not know which to admire most, the tact or the courage of his approach to Nathanael. His friend is a scholar, a student of the scriptures, who would at least exact that the best known predictions of the prophets should be fulfilled in the Messiah. Philip announces with conviction, 'We have found Him of whom Moses in the Law and the prophets did write,' for this was the appeal which would reach his friend; and yet in the same breath he admits that two of the most familiar Messianic prophecies are *not* fulfilled in the man whom he calls the Christ. Every Jew knew that out of Bethlehem should come the Messiah,[74] and that His birth should be unique among men, for 'behold, a *virgin* shall conceive and bring forth a son.'[75] The attitude of this new disciple is instructive to us. He does not evade the difficulty, nor slur it over, nor explain it away. He states on the one hand what would seem to him the irreconcilable difficulties, and on the other, his conviction, which is untouched, altogether unaffected by difficulties which to a Jew must have seemed insurmountable. This man came forth from *Nazareth* and was the son of *Joseph*, born like any other man, the son of a father. If we will receive it, there is a further lesson for us here, for the 'doubts' which intervene between the Light of the World and the hearts of men whom He should comfort, are born of our limitations and will vanish in the light of fuller knowledge, even of fuller scientific knowledge. Philip meets the reward of his faith. His friend does

---

passion for diffusing, for making prevail, for carrying from one end of society to the other, the best knowledge, the best ideas of their time; who have labored to divest knowledge of all that was harsh, uncouth, difficult, abstract, professional, exclusive; to humanize it, to make it efficient outside the clique of the cultivated and learned, yet still remaining the best knowledge and thought of the time, and a true source, therefore, of sweetness and light." Matthew Arnold, 'Sweetness and Light, from Culture and Anarchy', *A Library of the World's Best Literature* 2, ed. Charles Dudley Warner (New York, The International Society, 1896). 861-862.

[74] Micah 5.2.

[75] Isaiah 6.14.

not find these two mountains of difficulty insuperable, another lesson for us as to the force of conviction. The point Nathanael raises is an unexpected one. 'Can any good thing come out of Nazareth?' easy-going, pleasure-loving Nazareth, conceivably a sort of Naples of the East, a city beautiful for situation, set upon a hill, where every man sat under his own vine and his own fig-tree, where the beautiful children played as they play to-day among the oleanders, and red anemones, and swing gaily as they do to-day among the branches of the trees. To this objection Philip's sufficient answer is, 'Come and see;' and one hears the relief in his tone that this should be the only question raised by his friend. One is struck by the illustration of the offices of friendship presented by this group of young men, and we shall perhaps not go beyond the letter or the spirit of the narrative if we derive from it an infallible test of friendship which deserves the name only in so far as friend leads friend to the more perfect Way. One other reflection occurs to us. It is often spoken of as a mark of our Lord's condescension that He was born among peasants, though these were of kingly race, that He grew up in a cottage home in Nazareth, and that He chose His first disciples for the most part from a band of young fishermen of the peasant-proprietor class. But in the light of modern sociology we begin to learn that these are precisely the preferable conditions of life for a fine and enduring physical development and for vigorous and untrammelled intellectual force. We could cite numberless illustration from the great men of the hour, but perhaps another hill country whose peasant-born sons have distinguished themselves all over the world will make the point clear. Such names as those of Carlyle and Sir James Simpson carry conviction. In this, as in other things, our Lord was never exceptional. He followed and indicated a rule of life.

(v. 47). 'Jesus saw.' The regards of our Lord are always especially dwelt upon. He looked and He saw. In a more simple and perfect state of being we should all doubtless communicate with the eye instead of with spoken words. Christ saw and looked and read, with the perfect intuition which we have seen Him exercise before, the whole gamut of the character of Nathanael from its foundation 'An Israelite' to its individual development 'in whom there is no guile.' He recognised that exceeding subtlety of mind which descended upon every Jew from his father Jacob and which—even when combined with the piety and godward tendency that made the Jews the elect of the earth as holding for men the secrets of God—was not always without guile in its dealing with men. But there have ever been Jews with the spiritual insight, intellectual power, and moral perceptiveness of their nation, who are free from the hereditary tendency and guileless as a child. Such a Jew offers a singularly beautiful type of character and such a Jew our Lord saw in Nathanael.

(v. 48) He, with the astuteness of 'an Israelite indeed,' did not allow the pleasure of being so fully recognised to carry him away. 'Whence knowest thou Me.' How do you know this? Was his query; and our Lord's reply, enigmatical and unmeaning to any other listener, pierced his soul and told him that he was in the presence of the great Revealer who alone knows what is in man. 'Before Philip called thee, when thou was under the fig tree, I saw thee.' Every Jew has his place of prayer, be it the house-top or the closet, or, in our Lord's case, the mountain-top; or his own fig tree trained probably into a bower. There is that in each of us which is our very best, better than our acts or words or our resolution, our aspirations. The suffusion of consciousness in Nathanael would seem to show that Christ had surprised him in aspirations after the highest which he could disclose to no man: we may well believe that his thought had been of the coming One, for it is according to our desires, even according to our aspirations, that God deals with us. He knew himself to be in the presence of the Revealer of secrets, the Judge who came not to condemn but to show to every man the best that is possible to him, the unsuspected good that is in Him.

SCALE HOW 'MEDITATIONS'
Dominus Illuminatio Mea

No. 7 (*Continued*)[76]

(S. John 1:49-50)

(v. 49) Another *credo* follows. 'Thou art the Son of God, Thou art the king of Israel.' In this narrative we have the distinction between that intuitive perception for character which belongs to all sincere and simple persons, including children and 'savages,' as well as to the wise and learned who have still the grace to be simple, and that divine attribute of our Lord's whereby He is the revealer of men to themselves and the revealer of the Father to His children. A true and simple man might have pronounced that Nathanael was an Israelite without guile; only the Omniscient was with Nathanael under the fig tree.

(v. 50) More light is ever the reward of those who see. Nathanael receives the promise of fuller revelation. 'Ye,' not only Nathanael, but Philip, 'shall see heaven opened and the angels of God ascending and descending upon the Son of man.' The allusion to Jacob's ladder was perfectly familiar. The exquisite story had doubtless touched the hearts of both men. That was exactly what their heart hungered for—a ladder, a bridge, a means of constant communication and commerce between God in heaven and man on earth, whereon the angels could come an go; and Christ promises to unfold the mystery His two-fold relation, His close brotherhood with man and fellowship with God, which should bridge over all sense of distance and lift men as upon a ladder to their Father in heaven.

---

[76] Charlotte Mason, *The Parents' Review* 19, no. 5 (May 1908): 467-468.

SCALE HOW 'MEDITATIONS'
Dominus Illuminatio Mea

No. 8 [77]
March 20th, 1898

THE MARRIAGE IN CANA OF GALILEE
(S. John 2:1-11) [78]

(v. 1) 'The third day there was a marriage in Cana of Galilee.' This story has ever been especially dear to the heart of Christendom. It is, as it were, the benedictory smile of our Lord upon all Christian nuptials, and it affords promise of the sanction of His presence at all happy, simple, social gatherings. It is the first note of the teaching which proclaims again and again that the religion of Christ is, in truth, joyous and light-hearted: and that the sober sadness which some of us associate with our religious profession suggests an element of distrust. We have one other mention of Cana of Galilee as the city of Nathanael, of whose call we have been reading[79] Two sites, both within easy distance of Nazareth, are both claimed as Cana. 'The mother of Jesus was there,' apparently as an honoured guest, perhaps a kinswoman.

(v. 2) 'Jesus was bidden' and the five newly-called disciples who had begun that course of literally following their Master which was customary in the East as well as in the West. We observe that Christ, with royal graciousness, accepts every invitation that reaches Him.

---

[77] *The Parents' Review 19*, no. 5 (May 1908): 468-471.

[78] Themes: Joyous religion of Christ; Parents; young people; authority; miracles.

* S John 21:2.

(v. 3) 'The wine failed.' No greater disgrace could happen to the abounding hospitality of the East. A wedding-feast still lasts for some days, perhaps for a week. All comers are entertained, not only invited and honoured guests, but the poor and the halt and the stranger within the gates share in the bounty of the feast. Small wonder that the wine failed. The mother of Jesus, who, we may believe, was waiting with intense expectation for some fulfilment of the great promise she had with her son, thought that here was His opportunity. 'They have no wine,' she said, not asking anything, but stating the need, which was her need also, in her sympathy with her embarrassed hosts.

(v. 4) 'Woman, what have I to do with thee?' We wonder as we read, and the explanation that this form of address is friendly and even tender in the East does not do away with the fact that it places the Virgin Mother at a certain remoteness form her Son; that is, however deep she is in His love, she is not any more in His counsels. We can see how inevitable and how tender was this decision of the Son of man, and how it saved all the jarring of contrary will and opposing aims which spoils the peace of many a home. Would it not be well if young people who are of an age to form opinions, and who find in themselves aims, desires, modes of thought, which are not those of their parents, should frankly talk the vexed question over with father or mother; and, with all reverence and gentleness, beg to be allowed to go their own way, so long as it is a good and right way. There are few parents who would not respond to such an act of frankness and real dutifulness; and the misery of households divided, not only in purpose but in heart, would be avoided by the simple following of our divine example. 'Mine hour is not yet come.' His time may be late, or so soon as to be almost immediate; intervals of time do not count in the divine mind.

(v. 5) 'Whatsoever He saith unto you, do it.' How well the Mother understood her Son. What perfect reticence and dignity and sympathy she shows. She is conscious of no rebuff, but waits the event. Her position of authority in the house is interesting; she gives orders to the servants.

(v. 6) 'Six water pots of stone. It is a curios fact that in one of the supposed sites of Cana in Galilee, a number of huge stone vessels, to hold about thirty gallons each, have recently been discovered. Just such water pots, we may suppose, were collected for the wedding. Jewish ritual demanded much purifying, washing of platters and of hands, during the progress of the feast; and no doubt, one special preparation for the wedding was the laying in of a large supply of water which could be drawn off as it was wanted.

(v. 7) Already, we may suppose, a good deal of water had been used. The kingly largess was to be bestowed with no niggard hand. 'fill the water pots,' and the servants with right good will filled them to the brim. 'Draw out now.' There are no steps in the miracle, no point at which we can say, 'then it happened.' We only know that water went in and wine came forth. The ruler of the feast seems to have been a friend who acted the part of master of ceremonies.

(v. 9, 10) He expresses his opinion of the wine in a popular proverb, but feels no surprise as he supposes that this wine also comes from the same source as the rest. The servants knew, but an eastern servant is a 'Caleb Balderstone'[80] to whom the credit of the family is everything; of course they would not betray the facts. We all know Tintoretto's *Marriage in Cana*, with the beautiful (Venetian) ladies, and the amazed guests, and the general sense of stir and *éclat*[81] about the miracle; but we get no hint of the kind in the narrative.

---

[80] Caleb Balderstone was a fictional aged butler of a house fallen on hard times. In a desperate attempt to maintain the dignity of the family, he resorted to comical and absurd actions such as smashing crockery so that guests could not be served any meals. Sir Walter Scott, *The Bride of Lammermoor*.

[81] French, brilliance: Great brilliance, as of performance or achievement. Conspicuous success. Great acclamation or applause.

(v. 11) We are told as the only result of the miracle that 'His disciples believed on Him'—believed more, that is, for living faith is ever feeding and growing from more to more. 'This beginning of His signs.' The Revised Version gives us 'signs' instead of 'miracles,' and the change is significant. A miracle is a portent, a marvel. The beholders wonder at it and their thoughts go no further. A sign, on the other hand, arrests the attention, directs thought beyond itself to the thing signified; and the thing signified in this case was the glory of Christ which he manifested forth that day. How? we ask. In the first place it was a kingly act of, has been well said, 'supreme courtesy.'[82] We, narrow and niggard of soul, can appreciate the grace of kindliness which saved the host from being put to confusion; but, we ask, with the man in the Gospel, why this waste? What need for perhaps something like a hundred and fifty gallons of wine for a single feast? But was it not a wedding gift, a supply that would last the family (on the choicest occasions) for a generation? And was it not also a mute witness for Christ; for, however unobtrusively the wonder was wrought at the time, the tale would be told a thousand times in the coming years; and among the future hearers there might ever be those who would accept the wonder as a 'sign.'

Further, this act is a 'sign,' as showing kingly power over what we call the forces of Nature; that very power which the Centurion claims for Christ when he prays Him to send His messenger Health to his house, just as he himself would send a soldier for servant. There is a strong inclination to-day to explain away, leave

---

[82] Julian of Norwich, a Benedictine anchoress (1343-1443) in her "Revelations of Divine Love" applied the term 'courteous' to God and to Jesus Christ: "But, [let us] beware that we take not so recklessly this homeliness that we leave courtesy. For our Lord himself is sovereign homeliness, and as homely as he is, so courteous he is: for he is very courteous. And the blessed creatures that shall be in heaven with him without end, he will have them like to himself in all things. And to be like our Lord perfectly, is our very salvaton and our full bliss." Julian of Norwich, *Revelations of Divine Love*, (New York, Cosimo Classics, 2007) 157.

out of consideration, the miracles of Christ; as being, anyway, unnecessary, not an integral part of His teaching or even of His sacrifice. A generation ago, the Gospel miracles were accepted as evidence, *proofs* in support of the claims of Christianity. To-day, they are proofs in quite another sense. They prove, test, the faith of Christians. Can we, in very truth, receive this history as a fact? Does the simplicity and courtesy and fitness of the act commend it to our hearts as just the very thing that Christ would have done? Well for us if this is so. For indeed the question of miracles is no by-issue, but is the *crux* of Christianity; we cannot accept the one without the other. This is a hard saying; but happily every one of us is provided with the means of testing whether these things can or cannot be so. Our Lord Himself gives us a scale whereby to measure the greatness of a miracle. 'Whether it is easier to say, thy sins be forgiven thee, or to say, rise up and walk?' The inward spiritual miracle commends itself at once as greater than any material sign. Wherefore, whenever we pray—'Give us our daily bread and forgive us our sins,' we concede the possibility of all miracles, for the lesser is included in the greater. 'Lord, I believe, but alas, I do not understand;' nor shall we probably in our present state of being. The doctrine of mystery is a wholesome one for the Christian soul. It is a doctrine which every scientist, every philosopher, has long ago accepted though he may refuse to apply it to the things of the Christian life. Who has solved for us the least of mysteries of birth and death and life? And why should we make a stumbling-block of the lesser mystery of 'miracles'?

SCALE HOW 'MEDITATIONS'

Dominus Illuminatio Mea[83]

No. 9

THE FIRST CLEANSING OF THE TEMPLE
(S. John 2:12-19)[84]

(v. 12) 'Went down to Capernaum,' *i.e.,* in the sense of going down from the capital. He went further north. 'He and his mother and His brethren and His disciples.' Our Lord had not yet had occasion to say, 'A man's foes are they of his own household.' We have here a picture of a united family group, in which the new disciples were included, attending the progress of the Son of man. We may read between the lines the glow of hope and promise the impulse of personal affection, which attended the opening of His ministry. Here, too, the son of man trod the way we all have to follow. Every earnest worker has known what it is to begin buoyed up by the faith of some fond hearts, and to drop his nearest and dearest one by one by the way, because they cannot understand that the glory which belongs to a divine mission is not ease and praise but continual sacrifice. Let us rejoice when in this also we are called upon to tread in His steps.

'Not many days.' The Synoptics Gospels record a lengthened stay in Capernaum, 'his own city,' 'his own country.' But the order of events as given in the fourth gospel is generally accepted. S. John takes up the record after the temptation with the testimony of the Baptist, and he alone tells us of the first Passover, the public opening, as it were of our Lord's ministry.

(v. 13) It is probable that Jesus had gone up with His people to

---

[83] Mason, *The Parents' Review* 19, no. 8 (August, 1908): 626-629.

[84] Themes: Work; sameness of work.

each Passover since his twelfth year. But now He goes, officially as it were, to take up His work as Messiah.

(v. 14) 'Those that sold oxen and sheep and doves and the changers of money.' We need not imagine that the desecration of the temple was so great even as that of Old S. Paul's where the nave was used as a common thoroughfare for cattle, horses, and foot passengers. There is probably no building in existence magnificent enough to aid our conception of the temple of Herod in all its new splendour. The plan was the same as for the tabernacle and the earlier temples—a Holy of Holies, a holy place, and an outer court. The last was surrounded by cloisters, and these were supported on innumerable Corinthian pillars of white marble nearly forty feet high. It was these cloisters which were appropriated by the astute priests and rulers to uses which they would, no doubt claim belonged to the worship of God. For was it not a kind office to have close at hand the animals needed for sacrifice, the coinage required for tribute, so that worshippers from afar could supply themselves at the least cost of time and trouble? We need not ask how far the coffers of the temple and the income of the priests gained by this means.

(v. 15) The Lord of the temple came to His temple and He pronounced judgment. He came in the majesty and power of a King. His instrument of chastisement was no more than a scourge of small cords, but no man dare resist Him, no beast might turn upon Him. We see the money-getting crowd driven forth by this one Man, not even daring to stoop and gather up the precious coins scattered on the pavement. We can believe that S. John as he wrote had before him his apocalyptic vision of the wrath of the Lamb.

(v. 16) 'Make not My Father's house a house of merchandise.' As usual, in the great crises of His life, our Lord decrees the principle upon which He acted. He sweeps off the web of hypocrisy, all pleas for making the offices of religion easier for the people, supporting more worthily the worship of God, and so on. 'there is no justification,' He seems to say, 'for exchange and barter concerning the things of God and in the House of God.'

(v. 17) 'The zeal of Thine house shall eat me up.' His disciples *remembered* what the Psalmist had written.[85] How we perceive the aged Evangelist recalling the flash of recollection and conviction which came to his soul as he watched Christ in the temple, and; 'with the rapture of a sudden thought,'[86] perceived that he was looking on at the fulfilment of a prediction which was one of the marks by which men might know the Messiah. We all know the feeling in some degree when we watch work, that of others, or it may even be our own, and suddenly perceive that the Lord is in presence, and that the work is being done by Himself, in His way.

'He went about doing good,' is a record of Christ's life which remains on every Christian soul. Men have argued that such work could only be done in the strength of a passion, and that it was in His passion for humanity that our Lord was strong, and hence that such a passion for humanity is in itself worship, the whole of religion. But every now and then in our Lord's life we get a glimpse, as though a mantle were blown back by the wind of his ideal, his hidden impulse, His enthusiasm, His master-passion, if we may reverently say so. It was not what has been called 'the enthusiasm of humanity.' That was the consequence, not the moving cause. 'My Father's business,' 'My Father's house'; in such phrases as these we get the key to the life of Christ. That men should know the Father, should live that life of serene passion and meek and lowly enthusiasm which is the final possibility of human nature—for this Christ came into the world; and every glimpse we get of His own 'zeal,' enthusiasm, may well be as fuel to the fire in our cold hearts. 'it is only as we live in the ideals,' says Bishop

---

[85] Psalm 69:9.

[86] Charles Dickens, "Dr. Bookley and His Wife" *Household Words* (London: Charles Dickens and Evans, 1884) 473.

Westcott, 'that sameness of work does not become monotony of life.'[87] We cannot escape sameness of work if we wish to effect anything. The greatest achievement evolves itself out of endless petty and unnoticeable details; but, thank God, we need none of us suffer from that last dreariness, monotony of life. One thought of God, one glimpse of our ideal, and we go to work with renewed impulse and quickened posers, remembering that all the power of Christ is behind every scourge of small cords with which we would cleanse the defilement or our own hearts or of the world.

This, at least, do we learn from the glimpse afforded of the personality of our Lord. From His action, the obvious lesson is the reverence due towards the house of God, the place of his presence: reverence in the care and worthy keeping of whatever is set apart for divine worship, reverence in our own deportment, and as we gather from the immediate turn of thought by which our Lord associates a building made with hands with that other temple of God, the human body ('Ye are the temple of the living God'[88]) We perceive that we are not allowed to think about our neighbours' bonnets, nor about the little peculiarities of the clergyman, nor about the thousand trifles so tempting to our inconstant minds, nor are we to think thoughts of traffic and barter, nor allow that inner temple of ours to become a public thoroughfare for worldly thoughts in hours and places consecrated to worship. Neither are we allowed to go about with our guidebooks irreverently and rudely in foreign churches, disturbing the worship of others.

(v. 18) The Jews, priests, and other, stand petrified. They perceived that a sign has been done before them. But have not the candour to accept it. They dally with their consciences, and ask

---

[87] "The average man, the man of business, the artisan, the miner, require the vision of the ideal, and they are capable of it. The vision of the ideal guards monotony of work from becoming monotony of life." Brooke Foss Westcott, *The Incarnation and Common Life*, (London, Macmillan and Co., 1893) 148.

[*] 2 Cor. 6.16.

for a sign from God to confirm that which had been done before their eyes. Our Lord, as ever, gives an enigmatical answer to the double-minded, an answer containing a deep truth which they were unable to read—the truth that a temple of God is at the best only a type of that other temple which every man carries in his own person, the temple of the body consecrated to contain the presence of God.

(v. 19) 'Destroy this temple and in three days I will raise it up.' In the days to come this was the one charge His enemies were able to maintain against the sinless son of man, that He had said this thing. And the saying bore fruit where alone it fell as a seed. His disciples remembered that he spake this when he was raise from the dead. The words of Christ sink deep, and this saying of the sanctity of man will yet bring forth fruit ten-thousandfold in the care of Christians for the ignorant and the sinful and the afflicted.

Dominus Illuminatio Mea [89]

No. 10

CONVERSATION WITH NICODEMUS
(S. John 2:23-3:1-15)

(v. 23) 'many believed... beholding his signs.' It would seem as if we were told of only one or two incidents of this period in Jerusalem. 'Many signs' may have been wrought. We are told only of the cleansing of the temple. This adhesion of 'many' now at the very beginning of His ministry should have been cheering to Christ.

(v. 24) but 'Jesus did not trust Himself unto them.' This seems to imply a popular demonstration in favour of the new teacher. Perhaps, as later, they wished to seize Him and make Him their king.

(v. 25) 'For that He knew all men.' It is not necessary to suppose that this knowledge was different in kind from the insight into character with which all wise and simple people are endowed. It was unnecessary for Christ to enquire of this one and that as to the characters of the people with whom he came in contact, and probably it is so with ourselves in proportion as we preserve the single eye. When we are 'deceived' in other, and complain that our trust is 'betrayed,' we may commonly trace our failure in insight to vanity, openness to flattery, an easy-going habit which is of the nature of sloth, or some other failure in simple and earnest living

---

[89] Mason, *The Parents' Review* 19, no. 8 (August, 1908): 629-633.

on our own part. These 'many' believers were perhaps too like many who crowd our churches now. People who believe in the sense that they have no intellectual doubts of Christianity, but who don't apprehend the nature an the power of that spiritual kingdom where in the whole nature of the Christian is brought in the obedience of Christ. We may believe it was the intentions of these men and not themselves which our Lord distrusted. Of the relation of all mankind to Christ it is true that He—

'Knows all, yet loves us better than He knows'[90]

(chap. 3) Thus early in His ministry our Lord brings us face to face with the great question of conversion. The anxious question of the hour amongst people of every degree of faith and unfaith is 'What think ye of Christ?' the controversy turns upon the possibility of recorded miracles, the inspiration and veracity of Scriptures. But the real question at issue is—does any power lie in Christ capable of changing the nature, habits, aspiration of a man, of even the worst man in the street? If Christianity can do this, it is indeed a lever with an arm of force enough to move the world. If it cannot, then men are right in saying, as they do say, that Christianity is effete. But is as well that we should all recognise what the real issue is, and that it does not turn solely upon ancient documents, however sacred.

(v. 1, 2) Here we have one of those brief, graphic introductions by which we come to know a man, with whom we meet in the gospel narrative, better than our neighbour whom we see every day. Nicodemus was a Pharisee of that sect whose observances we have learned to despise, but whose sanctity was held in reverence

---

[90] John Keble, "Twenty-fourth Sunday after Trinity — Imperfection..."
Christian Year.

> Stands in full sunshine of Thy piercing eye,
> But that Thou call'st us Brethren: sweet repose
> Is in that word — the Lord who dwells on high
> Knows all, yet loves us better than He knows.

by the Jews. He was a ruler, that is, a member of the Sanhedrin, the council or parliament of seventy, empowered to settle all matters connected with Jewish polity and religion, a Convocation invested with unlimited power so long as they did not come into collision with the Roman Government. 'He came to Jesus.' Our Lord's action in the temple had, we have seen, occasioned much disturbance of mind among the rulers. Possibly a special meeting had been called to investigate the matter. Nicodemus, with a sincerity which we admire, is not content to decide on hearsay; he will see Jesus Himself; but, alas, He comes by night. He has not the courage of his convictions, he does not choose to compromise himself in the eyes of the people. He would know the truth, but would not willingly give the sanction of his name to this new and uncredited teaching.

(v. 2) 'Rabbi, we know that Thou art a teacher come from God.' Here we have a further instance of candour. 'no man,' he allows, 'can do those signs which Thou doest except God be with him.' Again we wonder what the signs were which were done in Jerusalem at this time; they appear to have been numerous and convincing. 'we know' is significant. Is it that the beginning of the ministry was a day of grace for the Sanhedrin itself, that Nicodemus spoke of his body? If so, the mournful interest of a lost opportunity attaches even to the Pharisees.

(v. 3) 'Jesus answered.' As usual, our Lord fills up the hiatus between the spoken word and the unspoken thought. What is your intention? What do you propose to do? are you perhaps come to prepare the way for the Messiah? Such questions as these, hovering round the restoration of the temporal kingdom of Judea, our Lord would seem to read and answer. This kingdom is in the mind of Nicodemus. Christ replies, 'Except a man be born again, he cannot *see* the kingdom of God' Nicodemus looked for a kingdom that came with observation, with royal state and much observance. Christ goes straight to the heart of his error and tells him that for such as he there will be nothing at all to see; that in order to see this vision, a man must go through an extraordinary metamorphosis which can be described only as being 'born again.'

(v. 4) Nicodemus asks the questions which as we have seen, is the crucial question of our own day. 'Is it possible? Can a man again become an infant of days? Or as we would ask today, can a man change that which he is by heredity by confirm habit, by environment, and turn himself round and become someone other than he is? Is it, indeed possible? Our Lord reiterates His reply, but with a difference.

(v. 5) He indicates the power by which this thing can come to pass. The man must be born of water and of the Spirit. The idea of water would be familiar to Nicodemus it was customary for the disciples of philosophers to undergo a washing which was the sign of their discipleship, but this baptism of which Christ speaks was not only with water but with Spirit and with power. The out profession was necessary, especially necessary to such as Nicodemus, who came by night; and with it came the power of the new life in the spirit. A man must be born of water and of the Spirit to *enter* the kingdom of God. He must be continuously vivified by the Spirit to make progress in the kingdom when once he has entered.

(v. 6) 'that which is born of the flesh,' etc. Our Lord appears to read the struggle going on in the mind of Nicodemus, 'what is this that he saith; born of the Spirit? I know not what he saith.' The religion of this ruler was of practical kind, concerned with rites and ceremonies, things that a man could see; this new doctrine of a spiritual birth must have been strangely baffling and irritating. Our Lord considerably increases his confusion by unfolding the great principle which is the stumbling block of scientific men today. The laws which govern matter apply only to matter. The things of the spirit must be spiritually discerned. When a scientific man says, 'I can perceive nothing in the laws of nature which should lead me to the apprehension of the spiritual power you name God,' our Lord's answer to such a one is definite and to the point. Before he can see the Kingdom of God he must go through that radical change described as conversion or being 'born again.' There is no bridge, no easier way, for a man of philosophic mind like Nicodemus, or for the man of scientific training.

(v. 7) 'Marvel not.' This is not a subject for curious investigation, but for supreme conviction. Today we begin to see dimly the meaning of the mystery and to understand that God has made us so that there is an express provision in our physical structure for this marvel of being 'born again.' We know that a great idea seizes hold of a man, has power to modify the tissues of the material organ by means of which he thinks, has power to alter the whole course of his life. Many a man can put his finger on the moment of his inception of that idea which made him a poet a painter a philanthropist.

(v. 15) In proportion to the greatness of the idea and to the vividness of its presentation is its transforming power, and our Lord closed His talk with Nicodemus by presenting to him that master thought which should have power to subdue the hearts of all mankind—the idea of Christ lifted up upon the cross, as presented to the soul of each man with overpowering and all subduing force by the intimate Spirit of our God—'I, If I be lifted up, will draw all men unto Me.' The reason why any soul of man is not subdued before the love of Christ is that the idea has never been presented at all or that the presentation has been poor and inadequate. This, of the possibility of a new birth for every soul of man, however ignorant, however degraded is to be held by Christian people not in the region of intellectual calm, but as a passionate conviction of the heart. In proportion as we hold this creed will be the intensity and the success of all our philanthropic efforts, missionary or other. Nicodemus went out but, we gather, not converted. We read of him again[91] but the passage is

* S. John 7:50.

supposed to be interpolated. The last record[92]* is in character with the man. He brings species wherewith to honour the body of the dead Christ after another has already come forward to beg the body for burial. It is his way of saying *Rabbi* at last as he said it at first.

———

N.B.—The subscription for the second term is overdue. Will readers kindly send 1/- to Mr Middleton, Ambleside, without delay?

** S. John 19:39.

SCALE HOW 'MEDITATIONS'

Dominus Illuminatio Mea

No. 11

CONVERSATION WITH NICODEMUS

(S. John 3:8-17)[93]

(continued)

24th April, 1898

We passed last time from our Lord's saying, 'Marvel not,' to His prediction of that greatest event of the world's history —the lifting up of the Son of man—that marvel which should do away with other marvels and make the regeneration of the thief upon the cross a simple and natural event.

(v.8) 'The wind bloweth where it listeth.' The 'wind' and the 'spirit' are identical in the Greek and are translatable by the same word. We might say 'the spirit bloweth,' 'is born of the Spirit'; or 'the wind bloweth,' 'is born of the Wind.' But the change of word falls in better with our English idiom. Our Lord in His talk with Nicodemus goes straight to the *crux* of modern, as it was of ancient, thought. The religious formalist, like Nicodemus, and the devotee of natural science, two widely differing orders of mind, have ever found it unreasonable and impossible to believe and receive that which they do not perceive. They do not recognise in themselves, or in each other, spiritual beings expressed, so to say, in forms of flesh. Therefore they cannot receive it that the Spirit of

---

[93] Charlotte Mason, *The Parents' Review* 19, no. 9 (September 1908): 707-710.

God is in constant, most intimate, communication with man. They cannot [do] away with the necessity for the speaking voice, the seeing eye, the hand of flesh; and this saying of Christ's remains a dark saying.

'Where it listeth'—a poetic expression with the force of, free as the wind, as Shakespeare has it, 'a chartered libertine.'[94] But the little knowledge we have of the laws which govern the course of the wind, makes the figure all the more beautiful and appropriate. So of the Spirit, here and there, from unexpected quarters, to unlikely persons, ever moving, ever freshening, quickening, vivifying, goes the Spirit of God, and there is a joyous rustle when He comes among the leaves of the soul, and a voice of praise or prayer or thanksgiving, or an energising of the soul, as of branches in a storm, which is purifying and strengthening. But these are all secret things whose outer signs are only to be discerned by those who understand.

(v. 9) No wonder Nicodemus said 'How can these things be?' No word of Christ's has brought him any illumination as yet, and it is noticeable that our Lord makes no attempt to bring His teaching to the level of that formalism to which the Pharisee was accustomed. On the contrary, Nicodemus is chidden for his spiritual density. 'Art thou the teacher of Israel and understands not?' Prophets had spoken as they were moved by the Holy Ghost. Mighty men, strong in the Spirit, had arisen to deliver Israel. Nicodemus must, no doubt, have taught of these things; why did he not understand?

(v. 11) 'We speak that we do know.' 'Ye receive not our witness.' Here, for the first time, we have the division, the Church and the

---

[94] Shakespeare, *King Henry V.* Act 1, Scene 1.

> Turn him to any cause of policy,
> The Gordian knot of it he will unloose,
> Familiar as his garter: that when he speaks,
> The air, a chartered libertine, is still.

world, *we* and *ye*—The Church as yet so small, hardly half-a-dozen persons; the world—all the rest—so multitudinous. But the distinguishing sign remains. The church still knows those things which are spiritually discerned. The world, however sensible and excellent in other respects, still calls the things of the Spirit, foolishness.

(v. 12, 13, 14) 'Earthly things'; 'heavenly things.' Our Lord opens up such a vista in this and the following verse as S. Paul gives us when he tells us how he was caught up into the seventh (sic)[95] heaven and saw things not lawful for a man to utter. Not 'lawful,' not expedient, that is, because we are not yet able to understand. The love, the wisdom, the tenderness, the lowliness of our God, are baffling to the human understanding, and only he who descended from and ascended to, and, while he was with us on the earth, still dwelt in, heavenly places where the fruits of the Spirit abound—only he knows the measure of the unsearchable riches of God.

(v. 15) Our Lord closes the talk with Nicodemus by indicating that Event which would reveal to men, as never before, the amazing love of God.

(v. 16-21) It is considered that these verses contain the Evangelist's commentary upon this midnight dialogue. He follows out the thought to which Christ appears to have led Nicodemus up, that is, that it was the love of the Father more, if possible, than the love of the Son, that was manifested in the Cross; because, to give the 'only begotten Son' appeals to every parent and every person who has known what it is to love, as the supreme sacrifice, greater, if we may say so, than the death upon the Cross. A certain school of theology has in the past tended to obscure the Evangelist's teaching on this point. But any creed

---

[95] 2 Corinthians 12:2 "I know a man in Christ who fourteen years ago was caught up to the third heaven—whether in the body or out of the body I do not know, God knows."

which tends to magnify the love of the Son for sinful men as beyond that of the Father is hardly the creed of Him who came to reveal the Father.

'Believeth on Him.' When we 'believe in' each other it is truly that we recognise each other, know each other for better, for worse, and, because we recognise, place implicit confidence in one another. It is only by observation, meditation, and happy, intuitive sympathy that we know one another in this way. Most men and women we still see 'as trees walking'; it is only in the few that we 'believe.' It is such belief as this, intensified by every thought of Him who is 'altogether lovely' until it becomes the master thought of all our thinking, the moving spring of all our being, which issues in that constant and joyous commerce between the spirit of man and the Spirit of God which is eternal life, now, at the present moment, and reaches forward to those 'heavenly things' which it is not lawful for man to utter.

(v. 17) There is no thought of terror in the mission of the 'Son.' He comes to save the world; but even so, a natural, incidental, judgment is going on. Of their own accord men judge themselves, and range themselves into the sheep and the goats. To see the best and choose the worse, this is to judge oneself, this is to love the darkness: and people of irreproachable lives may conceivably prefer the darkness, for there is no middle state. That which is not light is darkness, and that shaking of the shoulder and repudiating of Christianity as an effete[96] religion, which is common amongst us to-day, what is it but a rejection of that Light, able to make manifest the evil—pride, selfishness, sloth—in lives whose goodness passes current in the world. For those who come to the Light there is no judgment; the tendency of their lives is revealed by the Light; they sin, but thy sorrow for it; and dread above all things the withdrawal of the Light by which they live. So, too, when they 'do the truth' there is no elation, none of that self-

---

[96] No longer capable of producing young; infertile; barren; sterile.

magnification which is of the nature of sin, because they come to the Light that their works may be made manifest that they have been *wrought in God.* They do not covet the praise of well-doing, but the far more joyful promotion of being co-workers with the Highest, through whom He condescends to work.

Dominus Illuminatio Mea

No. 12

THE LAST WITNESS OF THE BAPTIST

(S. John 3:22-4:4) [97]

1st May, 1898

(v. 22) Jesus and His disciples came into the land of Judea out of Jerusalem as we might say we go into Middlesex out of London. 'Tarried with them'—a pleasant suggestion of rest and converse after the ministry at Jerusalem (*cf.* 'Come ye apart into a desert place and rest awhile'). But now, as then, there was little leisure; crowds followed. 'and baptised,'—noticeably, immediately after the teaching given to Nicodemus about baptism.

(v. 23) Here we have the suggestion of another encampment by the Jordan. Ænon was considerably further north than our Lord's station in Judea, six or eight miles to the south of Galilee. The necessity for 'much water' appears to show that 'great multitudes' still resorted to the baptism of John, like the three thousand on the Day of Pentecost, like the ten thousand converts baptised by S. Francis Xavier[98] at Travancore.

(v. 24) 'John was not yet cast into prison.' The Evangelist only alludes to a circumstance fully recorded in the synoptic gospels, whose contents were, no doubt, well known to the Church.

(v. 25) 'Questioning' with a Jew about purifying. This Jew had probably attended our Lord's teaching about baptism on the

---

[97] Mason, *The Parents' Review 19*, no. 9 (September 1908): 710-713.

[98] Roman Catholic missionary and co-founder of the Jesuit Order.

banks of the Jordan. We are not told what He said on this occasion, but we gather from the gospels that it was His habit to fix new truths in His hearers' minds by almost verbal repetitions on several occasions. Our Lord's teaching appears to have been, always addressed in the first place to His disciples. They no doubt were present in that common sleeping-room where Nicodemus came to Him by night, and we may believe that He repeated His teaching as to the baptism of regeneration by the Holy Spirit here by the Jordan. Now the baptism of John was, we know, that of 'repentance for the remission of sins.'[99] There was nothing mysterious or divine in it. It meant no more than 'I am sorry I have done amiss and will turn over a new leaf.' But this sacramental Baptism with hidden meanings, out of which a man came a new creature, because the Spirit of God came upon his spirit, this was different. To the mind of the curious Jew two opposite sects would doubtless appear to have arisen.

(v. 26) The baffled disciples of John came to their master. They are a little sore. He that was baptised of John (and surely the less is baptised of the greater), He to whom John bare witness (and surely the greater bears witness of the less), He was baptising in Jordan and all men came to Him. This is the first measure we have of what *we* should call the success of our Lord's teaching in Jerusalem—all men, crowds, multitudes. The disciples of the Baptist are a little like furious school boys, with their 'It's a shame,' 'it's not fair.'

(v. 27) The Baptist answers with one of those words of marvellous insight, expressed with the terseness and force of an epigram, which make him perhaps a more distinct and powerful personality to us than is either of the apostles. 'A man can receive nothing except it hath been given him from heaven.' For the present difficulty, how sufficient an answer! If 'all men' go to Christ, it is because God so wills it. May a teacher sent from God

---

[*] S. Luke 3:3.

object to the will of God? What an illuminating maxim for us—a teaching of peace and acquiescence in all the circumstances of our lives! If we seem to ourselves to have been called to a special piece of work in God's world and to have been graced with great success, what heart-burnings arise when somehow the work passes out of our hands into those of another. But what can we say, how can we resent and rebel, how can we fume and fret, when we realise that 'a man can receive nothing except it be given him from heaven'? It may be that the other is more fit than ourselves. It may be that we have spoiled our work by some form of vanity or other display of egotism. Anyway, we bow with sincere submission to the decision that comes from above.

Again, this saying of the Baptist's sheds lustre on every little detail of joy and blessing that comes into our lives. It is so good to know that these things are *given* one by one. And again in failure, disappointment, when we are humiliated by reproof, apparently unjust reproof, how the irritation of our spirit is soothe when we recollect that,—

'Shimei's stone and Shimei's curse
Are kind rebukes from Thee.'[100]

(v. 28) 'I said I am not Christ.' This appears to point to an effort on the part of the Baptist's disciples to exalt him unduly and to receive him as the promised Messiah. He is able to refer them to his own consistent denial.

---

[100] John and Charles Wesley, *the Poetical Works of John and Charles Wesley* 9 (London: Wesleyan-Methodist Conference1870) 171.
536. The Lord hath said unto him, Curse David.—xvi. 10.

Lord, I adore Thy righteous will,
Through every instrument of ill
My Father's goodness see,
Accept the complicated wrong
Of Shimei's hand, and Shimei's tongue.
As kind rebukes from Thee.

(v. 29) Here, for the first time, we have the exquisite figure of the Church as the Bride. 'the Church,' no longer the 'we' of the conversation with Nicodemus, but the 'all men' who came for baptism. Instead of chagrin and envy the Baptist has the joy of the friend of the bridegroom. In the rumour that many people came to the teaching of Christ, he hears the Bridegroom's voice.

(v. 30) Here we have again an epigrammatic saying in which is contained the whole law of the progress of the Christian life: 'He must increase, but I must decrease.' It applies in the first place to John's popularity and apparent success as a teacher. But in these words we find also the blessed law, 'less of self, and more of Thee'[101] which Christian people find fulfilled in themselves to their great ease in living. There is no greater compensation for the freshness of youth with its keen pains and exquisite joys than the greater sense of simple, natural, inevitable dependence that comes in later life, together with that rather pathetic humility which is no longer shocked at fall or failure because it has ceased to expect anything good of self and waits upon Christ for every goodness and every grace.

(v. 31, 36) Bishop Westcott regards these verses as the comments of the Evangelist upon the witness of the Baptist. It is practically an echo of the conversation with Nicodemus, with however, a special indication to the particular case in point. 'He that cometh from heaven is above all.' Christ has already expanded this thought. It was He who descended out of heaven and ascended into heaven. John is of the earth and speaketh of the earth; his baptism belongs to things of the earth which all men

---

[101] Hymn: *O The bitter Shame and Sorrow*:

> Day by day His tender mercy,
> Healing, helping, full and free,
> Sweet and strong, and ah! so patient,
> Brought me lower, while I whispered,
> "Less of self and more of Thee."

can understand.

(v. 32) Again the Evangelist re-echoes our Lord's words (S. John 3:2) But he uses the singular 'He' instead of the plural 'we.' Our Lord came to bear witness, to reveal to us those things which no man can see.

(v. 33) 'Hath set to His seal that God is true.' The reference appears to be to the prophetic teaching which all men accepted but no man applied; those who saw it fulfilled in Christ recognised the truth of God. 'He giveth not the spirit by measure.' The reference is to Isaiah 61.2 'the Spirit of the Lord God is upon me, because the Lord hath anointed me to preach good tidings unto the meek; He hath sent me to bind up the broken hearted, to proclaim liberty to the captives, and the opening of the prison to them that are bound.'

(v. 35) The Evangelist again enforces the truth of the united action of the Father and of the Son.

(v. 36) Again we have a repetition of our Lord's words about eternal life. 'He that believeth on the Son hath eternal life,' now, at the present moment. 'obeyeth' and believeth' are, as it were, synonymous; for that entire recognition of our Lord's person and work in which eternal life—love, joy, hope, perfect peace—begins, must needs lead to obedience. 'He that obeyeth not, shall not see life.' 'I can't see what you mean by new life, being born again, and so on.' The things of the Spirit are spiritually discerned. 'The wrath of God abideth'—the judgement of God which the sinner practically pronounces upon himself when he chooses darkness rather than light.

(Chap. 4:1-3) Here we have an instance of our Lord's exquisite consideration for the feelings, not of John whose faith was strong but of John's disciples who were sore and vexed for their master. When Christ heard the rumour of His teaching and baptising which had troubled the disciples of John, He did away with the cause of offence by leaving Judea and departing again into Galilee. It is interesting to read that from the first our Lord received converts into His Church through His disciples, 'Jesus Himself baptised not, but His disciples.'

Scale How 'Meditations'

Dominus Illuminatio Mea.

No. 13

FOURTH SUNDAY AFTER EASTER
(S. John 4)[102]
May 8th, 1898

(v. 1, 4) We now come to one of the most interesting 'introductions' given us in the Gospels. We hear now of our lord's second visit to Galilee. He journeyed, partly that there might be no apparent rivalry between Himself and the Baptist, passing through the hostile country of Samaria, with its mixed Jewish and Babylonian race, between whom and the Jews there was undying hatred, for those whose help is refused will certainly hinder. The distance to Galilee through Samaria is probably a three or four days' walk.

(v. 6) The well of Sychar is still shown, and there can scarcely be a more sacred place, for this is one of the few spots that can really be identified. Our Lord, being wary with His journey, sat, 'as He was,' beside the well. The note of humanity is very interesting; and the hour of noon corresponds with an idea of weariness and thirst.

(v. 7) We may imagine the scene: the woman coming, poor, as the richer classes did not bear their own water, with bold rather

---

[102] Mason, *The Parents' Review* 19, no. 10 (October 1908): 785-789.

handsome face behind her veil, and when our Lord said, not to open conversation, but because He was thirsty, 'Give Me to drink,' dipping her vessel into the deep well; and we may imagine the pleasant gurgle of the water, His own creature, yet He would work no miracle for Himself, and relied on this woman's services. We are never told that she gave the water: we trust that she did, for the Christian feel envious of her privileges; but 'inasmuch as ye have done it unto the least of these... ye have done it unto me.'

(v. 8) The Jews could eat but little that a Samaritan had touched, without defilement, but the disciples could buy such articles as eggs or fruit.

(v. 9) Considering the nature of the woman and the feeling of the times, the woman's reply is comprehensible though churlish;[103] she would know our Lord as a Jew by His dress.

(v. 10) Mark the difference between the divine character of our Lord, and this neither 'nice' nor virtuous woman. We, when we receive a churlish answer, feel sore, think 'they are not capable of understanding,' yet our Lord gave His best and deepest teaching to her, pouring it out as to His nearest disciples. We are never told to 'cast our pearls before swine,' but our Lord saw that there was good ground in her heart in which the seed might grow and bear a hundredfold. Jesus 'answered' not her question, but what was within the thirst lying behind her flippant passionate nature and life of sin; thus the parable came to Him of the pure refreshing water and her need of just the same influence. 'The Gift of God' is life eternal, to know thee the one true God, Christ Himself.

(v. 11) We see the anxiety of the Samaritans to claim their Jewish origin and ownership of this well of running living waters, which is still a great possession, though its waters run only in winter. The woman was impressed by the manner and face of our Lord, and her memory wandered back to Moses, who *had* brought

---

[103] Vulgar.

water from the rock, and the saying 'A prophet shall the Lord your God raise up unto you like unto me.' Her attention is challenged, she thinks.

(v. 13, 14) Again Jesus answer the thought of her heart:— No, I am not going to strike a rock or open another fountain, but the water of life shall prevent the thirst of famine, and give the 'hunger and thirst after righteousness,' which is blessed.

(v. 15) The hot barren places of the woman's heart would indeed 'desire the water-brooks,' and yet she returns to her old flippant way, asking for a miracle to prove Him a prophet and not a dreamer of dreams; in a practical spirit, thinking of cares and fatigues, and ignoring any spiritual aspect; irritable, as people often are if their conscience and heart begin to be touched without being fully awakened.

(v. 16) This was 'a sign' to show the woman that He knew all about her, that she might not slip back into materialism. And here we come to the woman's grain of sincerity and truth, which drew Christ to her.

(v. 17) She acknowledges the faults of her life, showing herself to be a woman who had forfeited respect.

(v. 18) Our Lord had sifted the grain of gold from the chaff: 'thou hast said truly.' The law of divorce was then very lax among the Jews, and this woman was probably 'not easy to get on with;' thus she had sunk into sin. All our relationships with parents, family and friends are known to our Master, and He notes every sweet, kind, good and pleasant thing in our relationships; Himself the living Father and the tender Brother, ever ready with sympathy and compassion.

(v. 19, 20) We see that the woman is now convinced; she has been trying 'to make our Lord out,' and is rewarded for her pains. Yet she tries to turn the conversation by bringing up the great controversy between Jews and Samaritans.

(v. 21) The hour came, when at the crucifixion the veil of the Temple was rent in twain; for God has His times and seasons, and 'our times' for our country and ourselves are in His hands.

(v. 22) This is aimed straight at popular tolerance. There is none of the laxity with Christ, which says—

'For rival creeds let priests and zealots fight,
He can't be wrong whose life is in the right.'[104]

If we consider it the same to be a Samaritan or a Jew, and held religion to be a matter of climate and nationality, we should be exonerated from all missionary efforts, or desire to teach.[105]

(v. 24) But our Lord does not think deep teaching too good for this woman. The Jews worshipped in truth as formalists, but 'God is a Spirit,' and we must by teaching and thought have right ideas of God, that we may worship Him in spirit and in truth. Our Lord knew that no thought is too deep for any human being if it is only put in the right way.[106]

(v. 25) That spiritual hunger has now been awakened in her heart, she wants to know and understand, to see the Messiah (for the Samaritans had five books of the Old Testament and knew these prophecies) who will 'declare all things.'

(v. 26) He that seeketh, findeth; who knocketh, is opened unto. Our Lord makes His first great revelation of himself, saying "I am He," to this woman—honouring her in her need—who gave but a

---

[104] Alexander Pope, *The Works of Alexander Pope* 4 (London: Longman, Brown & Co. 1847) 114.

For modes of Faith let graceless zealots fight;
His can't be wrong whose life is in the right:

[105] Brief argument for the importance of a definite creed, rejecting universalism with the practical argument that it destroys the foundation for missions and teaching.

[106] Another principle for effective teaching, derived from Christ's example.

cup of cold water, yet received the revelation of the Messiah. If the Bible were not an inspired book[107] we should here have descriptions of her sensations and wonder, but with divine reticence we hear nothing of all this.

(v. 27) A Jewish woman would never have thus talked to a stranger. 'Rebekah at the well' is a type of modesty, and the disciples marvelled at this conversation with an evidently bold woman, but they revered their Master too much to dream of interference.

(v. 28) She was so interested now that she had forgotten the things of the world, as we are sometimes permitted in prayer to do when we forget intercession in thanksgiving.[108]

(v. 29, 30) We see the woman's character in her saying this 'to the men,' and we gather that she believed in her heart, yet feared to draw down their ridicule upon her. Because the salient feature of her life had been seized upon, she felt that her whole life was known, and she spoke with such conviction that the men went that long way to Christ. This sinner was the first woman-missionary.[109]

(v. 31) We return to Christ, whose disciples would minister if they might. We say of our interests that they are 'meat and drink to us,' and this is what Christ says: 'My meat and drink are to do the will of Him that sent Me.' Here we have another indication that not Christ alone laboured to bring back men to the peace of His kingdom. But 'God so loved the world,' etc., and to each of us is given the privilege of doing some little of the work Christ came to do.[110]

---

[107] The Bible is an inspired book therefore its writing bypasses that which is not relevant.

[108] This suggests Mason's familiarity with daily prayer.

[109] Mason often paid attention to the details of the role of women in the Gospel.

(v. 35) Our Lord was then 'waiving the first-fruits of the barley harvest,' rejoicing, with the joy of the harvest, over the soul of this woman and looking forward to the great ingathering of souls.

(v. 36, 38) We never know who has sown or who may reap. We may sow the seed of an idea, or reap its harvest in action and character. The prophets had sown, and apparently their seed was scattered to the wind, but the fact that some minds were ready to respond to Christ was because they had sown that He and the Church hereafter might reap.

(v. 39-42) We see the successful work of the woman, and read that one of the most beautiful and precious names of Christ, 'Salvator Mundi,' was given Him by those whom the Jews though of as outcasts.

---

[110] Mason makes here a reference to the work of evangelism.

SCALE HOW 'MEDITATIONS'
Dominus Illuminatio Mea

No. 14

THE HEALING OF THE NOBLESMAN'S SON[111]
(S. John 4:43-54)[112]
May 22nd, 1898

(v. 43) 'After *the* two days,' i.e., the two days He spent in Samaria. From thence our Lord journeyed north into Galilee. The reason is curious, for Jesus Himself testified 'that a prophet,' &c. Our Lord's use of this proverbial saying to account for His action appears to strike the Evangelist as it strikes us, with a little shock, and yet with a sense of gratification. Popular proverbs, which, so to say, embody the common sense of the people, are an expression of that practical quality which we least expect to find in our Lord. The mystic, the idealist shows every sense but common sense; he has no capacity for detail, and often spoils his life because he cannot conduct it to the issues he has in view. But our Lord's frequent adoption of popular sayings is a sanctification of common sense, an assertion that to use this practical quality in the conduct of our life is a fulfilment of divine law. This is especially to be noted by young people, who are not apt to glorify common sense. The more enthusiast would have remained in Jerusalem, and force his mission upon the Jews. Christ retired into Galilee, and gives us the reason.

'No honour' this is true in every day experience. Wordsworth

---

[111] Mason, *The Parents' Review* 19, no. 10 (October 1908): 789-792.

* In consequence of the P.N.E.U. Conference no 'Meditation' was sent out last week.

was 'a homely kind of man'[113] to the cottager at Grasmere; the greatest praise for White of Selborne was that 'he had no harm in him.'[114] It is, in fact, a happy provision. People who are doing great work can always find rest and retirement among their own people. 'Own country.' Our Lord's own country was Judea, the kingdom of the Jews, His chosen people, to whom he had just announced His mission in the cleansing of the temple,—'The Lord shall suddenly come to His temple.' He had found no acceptance. It was the aliens of Samaria and the despised Galileans who 'received Him.'

(v. 45) 'having seen all the things that He did in Jerusalem.' We only read of one thing. Here we have again a suggestion of many things. The Galileans, like the Samaritans, adhered to the Jewish religion, and went up to the feast. They would have two days to tell of the words and works of the prophet that had arisen in Jerusalem. Again we notice, as in Samaria, the readiness of the provinces to receive and believe when the capital refused and condemned.

(v. 46) 'He came unto Cana.' We may surmise that He came to 'water' the seed of truth sown at the marriage feast 'A certain nobleman,' officer or courtier, attached to the court of Herod Antipas, tetrarch of Galilee, a Jew, apparently, as was the tetrarch. 'Capernaum,' which came to be known as our Lord's own city, a thriving town in the fertile plain to the south-west of the lake, dear to Christians as having afforded a home to our Lord, but memorable as the scene of lost opportunities. According to

---

[113] Matthew Arnold, "Preface" *Poems of Wordsworth* (London: Macmillan and Co., 1882) vii.

[114] "every sound, became associated in my mind with the thought of the obscure country curate, who was without ambition, and was "a still, quiet man, with no harm in him—no, not a bit," as was once said by one of his parishioners." W H Hudson "Selborne" *The Contemporary Review* 69, (London: Isbister and Co., 1896) 279.

Christ's prediction, not one stone has been left upon another, and the very site of the city is disputed.

(v. 47) Here we come upon another of the marvellous silhouettes of the Gospel narratives. It would seem as if a spiritual searchlight were thrown upon each individual who comes before our Lord, and the whole life and character is revealed in a few sentences. This 'nobleman' is presented to us first as an agonised father, showing that depth and strength of family affection which is peculiarly a Jewish trait. His son was 'at the point of death,' and he 'besought' that Christ would 'come down and heal him.' 'When he heard,' &c. It would appear that he, too, had been among the witnesses of the many things that Christ did in Jerusalem, and, like many of us when we are driven to bay, he turned to Christ as a possible source of help. On reading the narrative we feel that, in his case, as in our own, such coming as this is an act of faith; but 'Christ meets him with reproof.'[115]

(v. 48) Our Lord speaks to him as a representative of his class, and as if he already knew him and read the secret of his heart, the lack of effort to *will*. 'Ye *will* in no wise believe.' This *will* power is often referred to by our Lord. 'If any man *will* to do the will of God.' 'And ye *would* not.' This active *will* to believe appears to be the one condition enacted by our Lord. Men must bring the will; Christ will give the power, and by the union of the two the miracle of the new birth is accomplished. Let us note here the simple means by which great ends are accomplished. The satisfying joy, the fullness of life, which comes of the recognition of Christ, is to be brought about, so far as our part is concerned, by an effort of will. The unhappy thing is that few people recognise how the will of man works. They are content to believe that to will is to resolve, and

---

[115] H.W.T. "Notes on our Lord's Miracles," *Thirtieth Annual Report of the National Society for Promoting the Education for the Poor in the Principles of the Established Church Throughout England and Wales* (London: J. G. and F., Rivington, 1841) 415.

that there is a certain strength in such resolution which shall accomplish its end. Now, the fact seems to be that *willing* fulfils itself by an effort of attention. Let us fix our thoughts upon that which we desire to know or to do, and turn away our thoughts from that which we should avoid and we have the secret to *willing*.[116] Most people desire the 'joy of the Lord,' but they do not will, do not fix their regard upon the Person and work of Christ. We are helped in this effort of meditation by the suggestion of His creatures—the lamb, the Lamb of God, the sun, the Sun of Righteousness, the fowls of the air, and the lilies of the field, and the reeds shaken by the wind, and the corn in the ear and the tree putting forth its leaves; —these are things upon which He has looked, and of which He has spoken, and which by the very laws or our minds, should keep the thought of our Lord present with us.[117] 'Except ye see signs and wonders.' The object of signs and wonders is probably not to convince but to attract, to challenge attention, and this attention is the first step towards *willing*. If we *will* fix our thoughts steadily upon Christ we shall be surprised into such an out going of love and worship as we little thought ourselves capable of. But we must do our part. Vague aspirations are not to be mistaken for definite *willing*.

The nobleman recognised in our Lord no more than a worker of signs and wonders. He did not, as that other who said, 'Speak the word only,' see in Him the Spring and Source of life.

(v. 49) 'Sir, come down,' etc. We begin to know this man. He has need of Christ; comes to Him in trouble, and he would not have known to do that had he not been interested in what he had heard and seen. He was probably one of those men of the world who would to-day claim to be interested in all things, absorbed in

---

[116] This is the same view expressed in *Home Education* which follows the teaching of William Carpenter.

[117] This shows how meditation, the contemplation of the works of Nature may lead one to faith in Christ, by strengthening the will through attention.

none. His answer shows that his attention is fixed not upon Christ, or the words of Christ, or on the reproof he had called down on himself, but solely upon his child and his own need. He reiterates his request, 'Sir, come down ere my child die.'

(v. 50) 'Jesus saith,' etc. Here we see our Lord's tender graciousness, His heart going out in sympathy and pity, in the friendly, reassuring, 'Go thy way.' We can imagine, had they been English, a kindly hand would have been laid on the father's shoulder. He is sent away reassured—'Thy son liveth.' Now the man begins to know Christ. By speaking with Him face to face knowledge came, as it comes to us in prayer and meditation.[118] Had the man not grown in faith he would again have urged our Lord to 'come down.'

(v. 51) 'His servants met him.' We imagine the meeting between the man and the friendly slaves. He was probably a good master, and therefore his servants shared his anxieties with eager, eastern sympathy. 'His son lived,' translatable by some such form as 'is doing well.'

(v. 52) 'So he enquired,' etc. From his question we perceive that a complete change has taken place in the man's mental standpoint. He thought now, not first of his son, but of what Christ had said. His anxiety is to connect his child's restoration with the healing word that had been spoken.

(v. 53) 'Yesterday, at the seventh hour.' The answer satisfied him, and he and his house believed. At first sight the faith would seem to be sudden and superficial, depending solely on the healing; but the journey from Cana appears to have occupied a considerable time, and this man, like the thief upon the cross appears to have passed the hours, not in a fever of anxiety and hope about his son, but in the contemplation of Christ. We gather

---

[118] Prayer and meditation, for Mason, are primary means for teachers and disciples to acquire a personal knowledge of Christ.

that a complete change has been wrought in his mind. He has been 'born again.' His household shared his joy, as they had shared his grief, for great is the power of faith and great is individual influence.

(v. 54) The 'second sign.' Only this one miracle is recorded by S. John during that circuit of Galilee of which the Synoptic Gospels give a rather full account.

SCALE HOW 'MEDITATIONS'
Dominus Illuminatio Mea

No. 15

THE IMPOTENT MAN[119]
(S. John 5:1-16)[120]
May 29, 1898

(v. 1) 'A feast' of the Jews, not evident what feast.

(v.2) A 'pool' by the sheep market,—a reservoir surrounded by porticos or porches, a colonnade, which, like all public places of the kind in the East and in the South, was made the resort of the deformed and the diseased. But, 'in these lay a *multitude*,' because the reservoir seems to have been fed by a spring which had medicinal qualities. Eusebius speaks of the red colour of the water, possibly caused by iron, and it appears to have been an intermittent spring; hence, perhaps, the legend of the angel coming down and troubling the waters, interpolated into the Gospel narrative and omitted in the Revised Version. One is unwilling to give up the gracious legend which might serve to remind us that when we derive health from medicinal springs, the spring itself is a divinely-sent messenger of health.

(v. 5) 'A certain man.' As ever, Christ singles out the individual for His divine dealings. We again watch the revelation of personality brought vividly before us under the searching rays of the Light of the world. Our first thought is compassion—eight and

---

[119] Themes: health from medicinal springs, the spring itself is a divinely-sent messenger of health; the revelation of personality brought vividly before us under the searching rays of the Light of the world; Will.

[120] Mason, *The Parents' Review* 19, no. 11 (November 1908): 855-858.

thirty years, a lifetime, during which the man lay as a log, perhaps for many years amongst those others—sick, blind, halt, withered. Many have seen in this concourse types of the spiritual condition of the world which Christ came to save; the sick, those who are weary of the world and of all that life offers; the blind, those whose eyes are sealed to the vision of Christ, and open only to the material revelations of science; that halt, those whose progress in the higher life is slow and distressing; and the withered, those who are insensible, who have no stirrings of aspiration, no regrets, no repentings.[121]

(v. 6) For all of these, as for this man, Christ has one question— *Wouldest* thou be made whole?'[122] He, Who came for the healing of the nations, makes one condition—the active *will*. 'Heigho! I wish I were a better man' or a 'better woman'—does not count. Nothing but that strenuous bending of the attention, which we have seen to be the mode in which the will acts, can fulfil the conditions. We all know of people who continue in bodily illness because they have not sufficient power of self-discipline to use the means of cure. They *will* not take the necessary exercise, or air, or food. So, too, of the spiritual life, though the Bread of Life, and the Water of Life, and the light of the Life, are brought to our very doors, though He stand at the door and knock. We must eat, we must drink, we must open, that is, we must turn our thoughts steadfastly upon Him Who is our salvation, and He will meet the willing will and fill us with Himself.[123]

---

[121] Mason suggests how many sicknesses may be interpreted as sacramental symbols reflecting spiritual conditions.

[122] Once more Mason highlights the importance of the will.

[123] Here meditation is associated with the discipline of the active will. The act of 'willing' fixes attention upon Christ. This is the necessary condition for humans to be nourished by him. In this light it may be understood why education, viewed as a process of strengthening the disciplined will, would be so important for Mason.

(v. 7) 'Sir, I have no man,' etc. The sick man takes our Lord's question as a reproach; instead of answering frankly, he defends himself peevishly. He says, in many words, 'it's not my fault.' In fact he has grievances— 'another steppeth down before me.'

(v. 8) But the patience of Christ is infinite. He is not repelled by the unlovely. 'Arise, and walk.' For the moment anyway, Christ succeeded in gaining the attention of this feeble soul. He looked into the divine countenance, some degree of faith came with even this slight effort. He was even able to obey.

(v. 9) 'He took up his bed and walked.' But we are disappointed in the man. He does not turn back to give thanks; there is no word of gratitude or recognition, no 'Lord,' not even 'Rabbi.'

'Now, it was the Sabbath on that day.' In this clause we have the key to the fact that henceforth the character of our Lord's mission undergoes a change. Hitherto He has been free to go and come, has been regarded with attention and interest, if not with faith; there has been no show of active hostility. Henceforth all is altered. His steps are dogged, His words are watched, He is, we may believe, worn and wearied with controversies, and the Jews go about to kill Him. He had not only made a man whole, but had bidden him carry his pallet on the Sabbath. This of bearing a burden, was an offence punishable with death by stoning. It would seem as if our Lord had gone out of His way to proclaim his controversy with the Jews. The impotent man would have been in his place the next day and next, and, even had he been healed on the Sabbath, was it necessary to carry his miserable pallet? As with Luther, when he nailed up his thesis on the Church door, there comes in the life of every reformer a moment when he must proclaim his controversy with the world, and our Lord did not exempt Himself from this condition. First, in act, and then, in memorable words—'the Sabbath was made for man and not man for the Sabbath'—our Lord removed the keystone from the arch which held together the whole fabric of the Jewish ritual and polity. *We* lead, alas, a double life, social and religious, and it is difficult for us to realise how this act of Christ's should affect a people whose every-day whole life was ordered and bounded to the minutest detail by their ritual. The very existence of the Jews as a nation, and their peculiar relation to Almighty God, would seem to their leaders to turn upon this question of Sabbath observance, upon which our Lord thus entered into open controversy with them. There was nothing for it but that the Jews must accept Christ or repudiate Him and seek His life. Henceforth no middle course was open to them 'One like unto a son of Man' had come amongst them, 'and out of His mouth proceeded a sharp, two-edged sword[124] for the dividing asunder of spiritual worship and mere ritual.[125]

(v. 10) 'the Jews said unto Him,' etc. The Jews attack the man whom they catch in the unlawful act, but we may believe that their desire was to find the worker of this untoward miracle.

(v. 11) 'He that made me whole,' etc. One reads the words at first with some relief as an expression of loyalty, but the rest of the story condemns the man. Again he says—'it's not my fault.' He hastens to excuse himself and lay the blame on another, though that other had been to him a saviour.

(v. 12) 'Who is the man?' One sees the keen, eager faces of the questioners as they catechised the healed man. The zest of pursuit is in their tones. Already the tragedy which ended on Calvary has begun.

(v. 13) 'Wist not who it was.' 'Conveyed Himself away.' It would appear as if our Lord's action were very sudden. Before the man had so far come to himself as to look about him and ask questions Jesus had conveyed Himself away, disappeared in the throng, for

---

* Rev. 1:13 and 16.

[125] Mason identifies the Word of Christ as the key to distinguish between mere ritual and true spiritual worship.

there was a 'multitude in the place.'

(v. 14) The persistency with which a human soul is put through its trial, its testing before God, is well shown in the sequel. The trial of the man so far has taken the shape of an amazing miracle of mercy. He had been found wanting, but Christ does not give him up nor let him alone. 'Jesus findeth him in the temple'; 'findeth' implies after having sought. Christ in the very crisis of His life had made leisure to go after this single unworthy soul. Again he has a trial which is his opportunity. 'Thou art made whole... sin no more.' Generosity had roused no gratitude. How will he answer to the test of rebuke? We all know that there are few surer tests of character than the way rebuke is sustained. The meek, frank soul accepts reproof with unclouded brow and simple gratitude; the ungentle soul resents. 'Lest a worse thing befall thee.' The worse thing did befall him instantly; he added vindictiveness to resentment, and went and told the Jews 'it was Jesus which had made him whole.' We try in vain to think that he did this thing in ignorance. A man could not have lived, as he had, apparently, upon the pity and the alms of the public without becoming a shrewd reader of countenance. He knew the law as all Jews knew it, and he knew well with what intent the Jews sought Christ. He anticipated the part of Judas and delivered Jesus to be killed.

(v. 16) We know no more of this impotent, for good to the last; but 'for this cause did the Jews persecute Jesus, because He did these things on the Sabbath day.'

SCALE HOW 'MEDITATIONS'

Dominus Illuminatio Mea

No. 16

TRINITY SUNDAY[126]

'As the Father so is the Son'

(S. John 5:17-24)[127]

(v. 17) 'My father worketh.' It is not quite easy to follow the argument, and see how Christ is answering the accusation of Sabbath-breaking. 'The Sabbath is sacred,' said the Jews, and Christ answered, And work also is sacred, for my Father, whom you call your God, worketh always, even until now, and I work. That work which is fitting and right is fitting and right on the Sabbath as on other days. The principle of Sabbath-keeping does not lie in the fact that the Sabbath is 'sacred' and work is 'secular.' Where it does lie our Lord tells us elsewhere, but here we have what we may call the sanctification of work, a doctrine which men and women are perhaps more ready to receive to-day than at any time in the world's history. We understand the blessedness of work for its own sake as distinct from wages, and the people who do work without wages are made to know that their work shall be at least as thorough and methodical as that of the wage earner, because the work should be its own reward, and in doing any task

---

[126] 'It is perhaps a little difficult to most of us to realise the fact which we commemorate to-day (Trinity Sunday) as the truth by which we live, and which affects all the relations of our life; sanctification of work.'

[127] Mason, *The Parents' Review* 19, no. 11 (November 1908): 858-862.

of hand or brain—however lowly—faithfully and dutifully, we enter into the blessedness of God. Community of work is Christ's first claim of equality with the Father, and in that light the Jews understand His saying.

(v. 18) 'For this cause the Jews sought the more to kill Him, because... he called God His Father, making Himself equal with God.'

(v. 19) 'Jesus answered.' The rest of the Chapter is occupied with a revelation of unspeakable interest. Our Lord's own setting forth of the conditions of unity and of diversity which exist between the divine Father and the divine Son. It is perhaps a little difficult to most of us to realise the fact which we commemorate to-day (Trinity Sunday) as the truth by which we live, and which affects all the relations of our life.[128] Our Lord's setting forth of the relations between two Persons of the Blessed Trinity—the Father and the Son—gives us insight and strength, and enables us to conceive what the Trinity in Unity and the Unity in Trinity may mean. 'The Son can do nothing of Himself,' &c. Our Lord first sets forth the subjection and obedience of the Son to the Father, the pattern of all true human subjection and obedience. The oneness of mind between the Father and the Son is so perfect that it is impossible for the Son to think, and therefore to do, a separate thing. Unity is strength and happiness; separateness is weakness and misery. We know it in our own lives. We know the soreness and irritation of soul that come to us when we are what we call 'cross' with anybody, even with a person indifferent to us. The more we believe ourselves to be in the right the more sore and miserable we feel, because we are forsaking the pattern of the divine Unity, and separating ourselves from even one of the people

---

[128] Here the church's liturgical year is revealed as an unacknowledged presupposition for the religious life at the *House of Education* and an integral part of its teacher training ethos. Mason acknowledges Trinitarian truth as the foundation of all relations of life, 'the truth by which we live.'

we know. The moment we think ourselves in the wrong, the soreness and irritation go. We are at one with our offending brother, and at one with all the world and at one with God in Christ. A little act of atonement has taken place which should help to picture to us the great Atonement; we bear the blame of the sin ourselves and unity and peace return.[129] Unity is power; we two are enabled for the best work only when we are at one with our fellows; let us 'keep the unity of the spirit in the bond of peace.'

(v. 20) 'for the Father loveth the Son, and showeth,' &c. This is a very gratifying saying. Even as a human son delights in the confidence of the Father he honours, so Christ would have us know that he too takes delight in the confidence of His Father. We are admitted into the secret of the divine relations; and human relations of love and reverence are strengthened by the vision.

'All Things.' 'greater works.' All things would appear to refer to the works of healing and help continually being done by the almighty Father for the creatures of His hand. Every parched lily of the field that recovers itself under healing dew, every sufferer recovered from his sickness,—these are among the 'all things' that the Father doeth and just such a thing has Christ done, only perhaps more immediately, in the recovering of the impotent man. 'Greater works' apparently refers to the three whom He will raise from the dead, thus prefiguring His own resurrection. 'that ye may marvel.' We have already seen that the object of miracles is to arrest the attention, and thus to turn men's thoughts to Christ.[130]

(v. 21) The Father raiseth the dead. Every life of plant or animal, every human life is a raising from the dead. Every stirring of the higher life in the human soul is a quickening. 'even so the Son also quickeneth whom He will.' 'Whom He will'—no arbitrary

---

[129] This presents the need for repentance for unity.

[130] Again, Mason stresses the relationship between miracles and attention to bring thought to Christ.

selection is, we may believe, implied but he that *will* to believe is he whom the Son *wills* to quicken. As in the work of the Father and the Son, so in the work of the Saviour and the sinner, unity of will is the necessary condition.

(v. 22) We have seen how the Son is in subjection to the Father in so far that He cannot separate His will or His act from the Father, because there is perfect union; because again, the Father 'sheweth,' teacheth, the Son. We have seen the equality of the Son with the Father, because, as the Father has the power of giving life to the dead, so also has the Son. Now we are told a diversity of operation, of a power which rests in the Son alone, the power of judging men. 'He hath given all judgement unto the Son.' 'For we have not' a judge 'that cannot be touched with the feeling of our infirmities, but was tempted in all points like as we are.' Neither have we a judge who watches and waits, and keeps the memory of our offences until the day of doom; but we have a Judge who condemns the transgression at the moment, while there is time to repent; Who reaches us as the Word, quick and powerful, able to discern the thoughts and intents of the heart.

'That all men may honour the Son even as they honour the Father.' How the Jews, who already accused Christ of blasphemy, must have writhed under the exceeding boldness of this claim! It would be impossible to put into words a more direct and unmistakable assertion of absolute equality; and yet, that which was the stumbling-block to the Church ever since. Now, men choose to honour the Father, and to recognise in our Lord no more than a very faultless man, our example indeed, a prophet even, but, after all, such an one as ourselves. Again, all honour is done unto the Son. 'Jesus only' is made the object of all love and of all hope, and the Father is thought of as giving a more or less reluctant consent to the great sacrifice of love accomplished by the son. When men honour the Father and not the Son, love grows cold; when men honour the Son and not the Father, reverence fails; and it is for our sake that our Lord claims this *equal* love, for it is only as we honour the Son, even as we honour the Father, that we can enter into the fullness of spiritual life provided for us and possible to us. 'He that honoureth not the Son honoureth not the Father which sent Him.' Our Lord here speaks in the character of an ambassador from Heaven in whose person the King is honoured or dishonoured.

(v. 24) 'He that heareth My word.' The allusion is, in the first place, to the word our Lord was at the moment speaking, then to all livings words of his gathered up in the Gospels.[131] But there is more than this; we live below our privileges. We are too apt to think that the commerce of speech between ourselves and our blessed Lord must be all on one side, that speaking is for us and hearing is for Him, that we may ask in prayer an He will answer in blessing; and this is true; but there is a more intimate truth, a fuller blessedness,—

> Well, if we pray till thou awake!
> A word, a breath, of Thee
> soft silence in the soul will wake
> Calm peace upon the sea.[132]
>
> (Keble)

---

[131] 'Living words' of Christ, connects with the initial thought of the meditation concerning life and Christ.

[132] John Keble: "Hymns for Emigrants," *Miscelaneous Poems,* 3rd Edition (Oxford: James Parker, 1870): 95.

No. 17

FIRST SUNDAY AFTER TRINITY
(S. John 5:24-29)[133]

'As is the Father, so is the Son,'[134]

We have considered so far how the divine Son establishes his equality with the Father—equality in subjection, equality in co-operation and equality in diverse operation. It is deep teaching, reaching the heart with a conviction which should affect all our human relations; and our Lord adds, 'he that heareth my word,' with that inner hearing of the heart, and 'believeth on Him that sent Me'—for He Himself is the Word, as it were the *utterance* of God to us—'he hath eternal life.' There is no judgement for those who understand and believe, because their unity with the Son is as the Son's unity with the Father. They comprehend His ways with men; they share his counsels; they further His purposes; they live His life; where there is this fullness of accord, judgment is impossible. They fail, and fall short, and mourn over their failings, because they are human, but their *will* is at one with His will; there is no separation. They *know* the Father and the Son, and this is eternal life; 'eternal,' not a joy reserved for further reward, but fullness of living now—'hath.' 'hath passed out of death into life'— as one passes out of one room into another, easily, naturally, instantaneously. We have all made the passage many times in our lives, when we pass from bitterness and anger and strife and soreness of heart into love and peace and joy and the

---

[133] Mason, *The Parents' Review* 19, no. 12 (December 1908): 938-941.

[134] Themes: All life is in the Father and in the Son; death; resurrection.

consciousness of the presence of God.

'Life.' Our Lord appears to be speaking in this connection of that liberty of soul, that vitality and joyousness of spirit, with which he speaks again when He says, 'I am come that they might have life, and that they might have it more abundantly.' It is 'more life and fuller'[135] that we want, that we crave sometimes with a sick craving; and we have a thousand ways of seeking that satisfaction which comes to us in only one way. Work, wine, art, pleasure, politics, the passion of love, all have been tried again and again, and have been found wanting. They give, indeed, the sort of galvanic life of the moment, which fails so soon as the stimulus is no longer applied. But life, no loner conscious of limitations, life of joyous, generous, expansion, free and gay as the bird's life, dutiful and humble as the life of angels—this sort of glad living is the instant reward and result of that recognition of the Son which we call faith.[136]

It is not difficult to distinguish between 'eternal' life and that life of the hour with which men seek to fill the void when the eternal life is not theirs. Eternal life is like the life of God, because it is the life of God. It is outgoing, generous, always giving, never grasping and seeking: nature and art, literature and history, all men every where,—these are its interests; these offer the wide field

---

[135] Alfred Tennyson, "The Two Voices," *The Poetic and Dramatic Works of Alfred, Lord Tennyson.* (Boston and New York, Houghton Mifflin Co, 1898): 34. 'Written in a period (1833) of great depression consequent upon the death of his sister.'

> Whatever crazy sorrow saith,
> No life that breathes with human breath
> Has ever truly long'd for death.
> 'Tis life, whereof our nerves are scant,
> O, life, not death, for which we pant;
> More life, and fuller, that I want.'

[136] Faith is defined here as the recognition of the Son, a necessary condition for glad living.

for its expansion. But the life of the hour, however fair it may be, is like the sea-anemone, all whose flower-like tentacles, spread abroad, not to give but to get, drawing food for the creature who is a mere sac, getting all things and not giving. We all know the pleasant-mannered, well-dressed, people in whose company we never touch great interests.

(v. 25) Our Lord will not lose touch with His audience. He perceives that this teaching of the deeper life has passed over their heads. They could not perceive or imagine a fuller life than that of the living, breathing, thinking men they knew themselves to be. Anything else they would have called mere mysticism, had the word been in their vocabulary. The 'Teacher' descends to their level, and with the solemn 'verily, verily,' amen, amen, the one form of asseveration He ever uses, Christ brings before them a manner of death with which they are too familiar. It is as thought He said—This life of which I speak to you is not a different thing, another life, from that which you call life, nor is the death I tell you of another manner of death; and that you may understand this, that your eyes may be opened to perceive the meaning of death and of life, the hour cometh when the dead shall hear the voice of the Son of God, and They that hear shall live.

Our Lord's allusion is, we may believe, to the three resurrections He is about to work, when the visible, fleshly bodies of the widow's son, Jairus' daughter, and Lazarus, should pass out of the visible earthly death and back again into the visible earthly life, which, after all, is only a part and a figure of the far richer, fuller, gift of eternal life.[137]

(v. 26) 'For as the Father hath life in Himself,' etc. Here we have the secret disclosed which men in all ages have laboured to discover. At one time this dream was of an elixir which contained the subtle principle present in every leaf of every tree, in the giddy

---

[137] Miracles are identified as sacramental figures.

whirl of summer gnats, as truly as in man, present everywhere, but for ever eluding scrutiny and test. To-day we think we have advanced because we no longer speak of the vital principle as an elixir but as protoplasm, the chemical contents of which we know all about, but yet are we no nearer the divine secret. Here it is revealed. Life, all life, is in the Father and in the Son; and whether the abounding glorious life which we call Nature differs in kind or only in degree from the free life of the Spirit, is a matter we know nothing about. Our Lord here draws the two together, proclaims Himself the Lord of Life.

'And He gave Him authority to execute judgment.' Judgement, like life, is not spiritual only, and is not physical only. But assuredly it is physical; we in the flesh suffer for every transgression of the laws of health and of purity. But judgment rests with Him who is also our life, and Who, because He is a Son of man, 'knoweth our infirmities, and remembereth that we are but dust.'

(v. 28) 'Marvel not at this.' Probably the derision of the Jews; and our Lord goes on to unfold that great mystery of the Christian faith—the general resurrection. There is no subject more baffling to human thought. On the one hand, our hearts assure us that those we have loved and lost must needs go on being alive, that the partings which agonise us cannot be final, and that, if we are to meet those dear to us again, it must be in the very form we had learned to love. We must see again 'the lineaments of gospel books'[138] in the countenances that have become dear to us. We

---

[138] Matthew Roydon. "Lament for Astrophel (Sir Philip Sidney)," *Songs of Three Centuries,* ed. John Greenleaf Whittier (Boston and New York: Houghton, Mifflin and Co, 1890): 7.

"A sweet, attractive kind of grace,
A full assurance given by looks,
Continual comfort in a face,
The lineaments of Gospel books;
I trow that countenance cannot lie,

must recognise the little tricks of manner and gesture by which our friend expressed that which he was. If we find him again, our hearts demand that we shall find the smile, the little gesture of the hand, the way he moved and spoke, 'our hearts know how.' but against this fond persuasion science has her irrevocable word. We know that that which we are will by-and-by move round with rocks and stones, will appear in the daisies that grow on our grave. Our faith is staggered more than need be, for this absorption of the material particles which go to make us in other lower live has been going on from our birth until our death, and it is no new thing that it should go on afterwards. How is it that the vital principle, the life, the self, shall make to itself that outer form which gives it expression in an instant of time? We do not know; we cannot even guess. But we do know that, given time, the years of our life, the thing *has* happened so. Every human soul has built up for itself that outer form which most expresses that which it is. We cannot understand how, but it is not impossible to conceive that that which it has taken years to accomplish with our low vitality and modicum of spiritual power may be achieved in an instant of time with the more intense vital conditions of the second life.

(v. 29) But we do not know, we see through a glass darkly. What it does concern us to know we are definitely told. We shall all hear the voice of the Son of man, and shall come forth, 'they that have done good unto the resurrection of life' to the fulfilment of all aspirations, the unlimited expansion of interests, to work, perhaps, which shall be without labour, and which shall accomplish its intent, to fullness of love and of light an of joy.[139] But we try in vain to understand; the heart of man has not conceived even a small part of what is covered by this word of Christ's—the 'resurrection of life.' They that have done ill unto the

---

Whose thoughts are legible in the eye."

[139] The afterlife will allow growth in the labors started in this life.

resurrection of judgement.' (R.V) May we believe that there is a note of hope here? They to whom the judgment of the Son of Man reaches in this life are self-convicted, and where conviction of sin is, is there not also hope?

SCALE HOW 'MEDITATIONS'

Dominus Illuminatio Mea

No. 18

SECOND SUNDAY AFTER TRINITY
(S. John 5:30-45)[140]

(v. 30) 'I can of Myself do nothing.' Our Lord repeats here the declaration of absolute unity with the Father with which this discourse began. We value independence, but we should do well to take heed that our independence is not separateness, which is of the nature of sin.

'As I hear I judge.' Here we have conceivably a reference to the Third person of the Blessed Trinity. 'The Spirit of the Lord shall rest upon Him, the spirit of wisdom and understanding, the spirit of counsel and might, the spirit of knowledge and of the fear of the Lord.' 'he wakeneth morning by morning, He wakeneth mine ear to hear as the learned.'[141] We may believe it is to 'the Spirit of counsel' Christ listens when He says, 'As I hear, I judge.' 'My judgment is righteous, because I seek not mine own will.'[142*] The gods of mythology have all one attribute—wilfulness, arbitrary action; they do as they like, because they choose. Man has made his gods after the image of his own heart; the undisciplined man, the ungodly man, is ever wilful. But Christ, in the very act of claiming to be one with the Supreme, offers in evidence the fact that He seeks not His own will but the will of Him that sent Him. It is for this that He can trust His own judgment.[143] Our Lord, in

---

[140] Mason, *The Parents' Review* 19, no. 12 (December 1908): 942-943.

* Isaiah 51:4.

** John 5:30.

this illuminating discourse, sets forth the arguments that prove his divinity. They are by no means such arguments as a man would have thought conclusive, but they are certain infallible proofs, and present to us an ideal only realised in Christ. They offer us tests, too, by which we may try our own character and motives, and by which we may know how far we are following in the footsteps of His most holy life. Here is a test for all our decisions, great and small. Are we seeking our own will? If so, our judgement is not righteous. Are we seeking the will of Him that sent us? Are we listening to that Spirit of counsel who abides with us also? Then is our judgment righteous. We may trust to our decisions, and go on fearlessly without regard to consequences.

(v. 31) 'If I bear witness of Myself my witness is not true.' Our Lord, like very orator who moves and teaches men, is following the thought of His audience. They apply to Him what is apparently a popular proverb:—'If a man bears witness of himself,' etc. Our Lord accepts a condition from which he, if any, might have claimed exemption; but, with that meekness which so often amazes us, he throws in His lot with us all, and confirms for us a saying full of insight. Here we have another of those tests of character which only Christ can meet. Our restless vanity will not suffer us to wait for others to discover our superior parts or possessions. 'I' is too often the theme of conversation. We are willing to admit that our talk about ourselves may be tiresome and may be boastful, but—'not true'? This we are hardly prepared for. It is worth remembering, however, and we may believe that we are so prejudiced upon the subject of our own achievements, of our own shortcomings, of our successes, of that personality which we feel has not fair play, that we are not capable of the simple, absolute truth in speaking about ourselves. We err by excess, whether in self-condemnation or self-approval. It is well that we

---

[143] Mason presents the paradox of submission as a solution for the peril of 'wilfulness' i.e. arbitrary judgment, the abuse of private interpretation. Solution: as Christ was submissive to the Father in his judgment, so should we.

should restrain ourselves from regarding ourselves, and then we shall not be tempted to speak on this difficult and dangerous topic.[144]

(v. 32) 'It is another,' etc. Our Lord's reference appears to be to the general witness born of Him by the Father.

(v. 33) 'Ye have sent unto John.' The testimony of John seems to have been a treasured recollection, and we may believe that every poor word of ours spoken in love and service of our Master is kept in His remembrance.

(v. 34) Our Lord is here referring to the witness of God, of which he is always conscious. We, too, have such a witness, for 'the Spirit itself beareth witness with our spirits.'[145] Whatever Christ claims for Himself we also have in our measure.

'That ye may be saved.' We unconsciously wonder as we read why our Lord condescends to unfold His own personality and His relation with the Father to these unbelieving Jews. Here we have the reason. He had none of the pride which scorns to explain but point after point, his argument is worked out conclusively. Our Lord's appeal is to the understanding of His hearers; a man might have appealed to their feelings, but He, who knew what was in men, knew that an idea received by the mind works itself out in the life, whereas a mere wave of emotion passes without a mark.[146] This is why our Lord's teaching is so often argumentative, that by all means He may *convince* men and that they 'may be saved.' The

---

[144] Mason recommends restrain on self-examination. She thought it improper to think and speak about oneself even for self correction. The "danger" is directly linked to the fall of man, which hinders our ability to preserve an innocent regard of ourselves. See Mason, "The Child's humility" *The Saviour of the World*. (Vol. IV):167. And, "The Fall—(The disciple)," *The Saviour of the World*. (Vol. IV): 173.

[145] Romans 8:16. The direct inspiration of the spirit upon every individual is a subject often highlighted by Mason.

[146] Here Mason rejects emotional manipulation as a valid source for discipleship.

opposite of 'saved' is 'lost;' lost in that ever-increasing hardness of heart which our Lord foresaw should culminate in the Crucifixion—the greatest crime ever done upon the earth. But the things Christ speaks of are things which they could not see with their eyes, things not demonstrable. He lifts reason above the plane of images received by the senses to the higher plane of those things which are spiritually discerned.[147] It is still true that we must believe with our understanding, with our reason; the things of religion must be received by the mind before they can be felt by the heart; and to the present hour the difficulty is that it is the tendency of the human mind to exercise reason only on the plane of things demonstrable to the senses.

(v. 35) 'He was a lamp that burneth and shineth.' For the second time our Lord bears witness to the Baptist; burning with that fire of God which we call enthusiasm, shining, giving light, because He carried the central fire. 'ye were willing to rejoice,' wherever the light of God is there is—

'continual Comfort in a face,
The lineaments of gospel books.'[148]

(v. 36) Our Lord cites another witness—'the works which the Father hath given Me to accomplish.' We are told of some of them, as, for example, the miracle which has just taken place—the healing of the impotent man. 'Who went about doing good'[149] is the

---

[147] Reason, for Mason, operates in levels, the outward level is that of perception, material, logic demonstration based upon such observation, the inner is the spiritual in which life, living ideas, are spiritually discerned by faith. Faith requires understanding but is not limited to its outward 'material' boundaries. The problem of her age was that it was exercising reason at the level of material reality, perceived by the senses, as the necessary condition for all knowledge including that which can only be discerned by faith.

[148] "Matthew Roydon's 'prescient estimate' of Sir Philip Sidney." in Alexander Balloch Grosart, *The Complete Poems of Sir Philip Sidney*, Volume 1, (London: Chatto and Windus, 1877), lxxxv – lxxxvi.

summary of the divine life given by the apostle Peter; doing good always,[150] doing nothing but good ever. Here is another of those infallible proofs which none but the Son of God can offer. And here again is a test for us who follow: by our works we are judged, by God and by man. The careful, humble, conscientious work, and the ostentatious, casual, imperfect work—there they are for judgment. We each stand or fall by 'all such good works as Thou hast prepared for us to walk in.'[151]

(v. 37) 'The Father... hath borne witness of Me.' Our Lord's reference here is probably to the voice heard at His baptism.

(v. 39) 'Ye search the Scriptures,' etc. Our Lord appeals against the formalism of their religion. They cannot discern what is said in those very Scriptures, which they all but worship, regarding Him of whom the law and the prophets did testify.

(v. 40) 'And ye *will* not come to Me.' Another pathetic lament over those *unwilling wills*, reminding us of the 'and ye *would* not' in the lament over Jerusalem.[152]

(v. 41) 'I receive not glory from men,'—another infallible proof. Who can say this but the son of man? The facile nature seeks popularity; the more strenuous, labours for power; and in one of

---

* Acts 10:38.

[150] A reference to Peter's address at the House of Cornelius: 'How God anointed Jesus of Nazareth with the Holy Ghost and with power: who went about doing good, and healing all that were oppressed of the devil; for God was with him.' Acts 10:38.

[151] This is part of the post-communion prayer according to the order for the administration of the Holy Communion of the Book of Common Prayer.

[152] 'O Jerusalem, Jerusalem, thou that killest the prophets, and stonest them which are sent unto thee, how often would I have gathered thy children together, even as a hen gathereth her chickens under her wings, and ye *would* not! Matthew 23:37. Mason 'willingness' is revealed in the Gospels as a requirement for the reception of the message of Christ's message. The will has a unique place in Mason's anthropology.

these two—popularity or power—consists the glory that comes from men.[153]

(v.42) Insomuch as we take to ourselves this 'glory' Christ knows us, and we may know ourselves, that we 'have not the love of God in ourselves.'[154]

(v. 43) 'I am come in my Father's name,' etc. This is true to-day. The person who comes in his own name, puts forth pretensions to genius, learning, skill, and what not, receives a cordial recognition; while the higher soul who is wedded to his art or his work for its own sake, to whom the simple doing of his duty is the sole aim of life, is not received, or the recognition he gets is tardy.[155]

(v. 44) 'How can ye believe?' At first it is not easy to see why a man cannot believe in God and receive glory from his fellows; but we cannot serve two masters nor worship two gods; this glory from men is the incense burned in that subtlest of all idolatries—the worship of self, and there is no place for the glory of God. What is the glory that cometh from God? 'I beseech Thee show me Thy glory,' was the prayer of Moses; and the answer was, 'I will make all My goodness pass before thee.'[156] In the face of Christ we behold all the goodness of God and the glory of God, but only as your eyes are purged from the film of self and anointed with the oil of the divine Spirit.

(v. 45) One more witness our Lord summons, even Moses, that

---

[153] The judgment of our work that really matters is God's judgment.

[154] Whoever cares for earthly glory, more than heavenly glory, does not possess the love of God within.

[155] This principle applies to Mason's understanding of the lack of recognition of her own educational efforts. Mason perceived that her work would be undervalued because it did not claim originality, but was simply faithful to the Gospel.

* Exodus 33:19.

very prophet whom the Jews were setting in opposition to Christ, and who pronounced their accusation; for they glorified Moses, but did not believe his writings, or they would have understood the teaching of Christ.

SCALE HOW 'MEDITATIONS'
Dominus Illuminatio Mea.

No. 19

THIRD SUNDAY AFTER TRINITY
Christ our 'Providence'[157]
(S. John 6:1-14)[158]
Part I

(v. 1) 'These things' include all the intermediate events of the second year of our Lord's ministry. We have the first event recorded when He went up to a feast of the Jews, probably the Passover, and healed the impotent man; then S. John leaves a wide gap to be filled up from the three Synoptic Gospels. The events include many miracles, as the raising of Jairus' daughter and the widow's son; the teaching by parables; the sending out of the twelve, and their return, wearied after perhaps a two months' mission, with much to tell and much to learn; and our Lord bids them, 'Come ye apart into a desert place and rest a while,'[159] Thus, in His character of His people's providence, providing rest and refreshment for the over-worked. May we not venture to believe that he himself was willing to share in the rest of the 'desert,' i.e., solitary place. We know the sequel—how Jesus and His disciples crossed the lake at the north to reach that other

---

[157] This meditation explains the importance of meditation upon the content of the teaching which one hears as the necessary condition for true education and growth in the spiritual life.

[158] Mason, *The Parents' Review* 20, no. 1 (January 1909): 58-62.

[159] 'And he said unto them, Come ye yourselves apart into a desert place, and rest a while: for there were many coming and going, and they had no leisure so much as to eat.' Mark 6:31.

Bethsaida, a scattered hamlet on the north-east shore; how the people saw Him go, and followed him by land round the head of the lake with such eager haste that they did outrun Him; how He 'had compassion' on them as sheep having no shepherd and 'welcomed them,' and 'taught them many things,' until at last the prudent disciples came with that conviction of their own superior common sense, which appears now and again in the gospel narrative, to counsel Him to send the people away that they might buy bread in the villages before night overtook them. S. John, the latest of the evangelists, tells only so much of the story, already familiar to the Church, as is necessary to introduce that teaching of the 'Bread of Life' which follows upon it, and which he alone gives in detail.[160]

(v. 2) 'they beheld the signs.' S. John adds something to the narrative. He tells us that, with the multitude, the signs which had been done had served their purpose: they had arrested attention,[161] filled the people with eager desire to see the Prophet who had done these things; as well as to serve their own sick, for he healed 'such as had need of healing.' Here we have two conditions of the spiritual life fulfilled; the people came ready to receive, and our Lord gave them freely of the spiritual food which ministers to eternal life—'He taught them many things.' We wonder how it was that the followers of Christ did not number many thousands of the faithful, instead of the handful gathered in the upper room, waiting for the coming of the Holy Ghost. But a third condition is necessary; men must not only attend and receive spiritual food, but they must assimilate it with some process answering to what we call digestion in the case of physical food; they must meditate upon what they have heard, ponder in their hearts, 'keep' it, live upon it.[162] Apparently this condition

---

* Mark 6:32-56.

[161] Mason often dwells upon the purpose of signs in Jesus ministry as a means to arrest attention.

was not fulfilled by the multitudes who listened eagerly to the words of Jesus; and perhaps the reason why many of us have to lament the little progress we make in the spiritual life is just this—that we attend and receive but do not ponder upon what we hear. We 'enjoy' a sermon, give ourselves up to a 'mission,' *feel* a good deal stimulated, our emotions are stirred; and, in a week or less, the whole thing has passed away from our thought; we recollect that we enjoyed and access of spiritual fervour; but make no attempt to keep up that living warmth. The reason is obvious; nothing comes without labour, least of all the things of God; and, having heard, we are apt to give ourselves no further trouble. We let the truth remain with us if it will, but we do not stir up our sluggish minds to keep it, go over what we have heard, point by point, many times, examining ourselves as to how far we are living upon the new truth or the new aspect of truth which has come to us.[163]

(v. 3) 'There He sat.' Apparently after the teaching and miracles, sat wearied, as upon that well at Samaria, because much 'virtue' had gone out of him.

(v. 4) 'The Passover.' The third Passover of the ministry, to which our Lord appears not to have gone up.

(v. 5) 'Lifting up His eyes.' How grateful we are to the tender love of the evangelist which saw and regarded these little personal acts of the Master. It is good and dear to the heart of Christendom to know that 'Jesus lifted up his eyes,' that 'there he sat with His disciples.' Why? We can hardly tell. It is as the little familiar gestures of those we love are dear to us; as Browning wrote; 'My

---

[162] Meditation, therefore, becomes essential for the spiritual life and education. Without it learning is not kept or lived upon, becoming unfruitful. Education fails when truth and life are not connected.

[163] This explains Mason's emphasis on meditation as a foundational discipline for her teacher training college. The discipline of continual meditation is at the heart of faithful discipleship.

heart knows how,'[164] of a gesture of his wife's.

Shakespeare expressed the feeling for us when he wrote,—

'Over whose acres walked those blessed feet;'[165]

he gives us the sense of the deepest love we are capable of, combined with surpassing reverence.

'Saith unto Philip.' This appears to be after the interposition of the apostles. Philip is honoured with an opportunity for a great venture of faith; and perhaps in the regard of Christ and act of faith is more vital and enduring than any act of service. How we wish it had been ours to answer—'Thou, O Lord, canst give them to eat.'[166]

(v. 6) 'This He said to prove him;' and, alas, Philip was proved—tried, tested—and found wanting. Is it caution, ineffable conceit, contrariness? What is it that hinders us when the opportunity comes for a generous response, a hearty confidence, if only in the mere expression of an opinion, to those who seek to be encouraged at our hands? We damp their ardour, we counsel caution, we pile up difficulties, nay impossibilities; we do not say—'Go and do the work thy hand findeth to do,[167] and God be

---

[164] Robert Browning, "By the Fire Side" *The Complete Poetic and Dramatic Works of Robert Browning* (Boston: Houghton, Mifflin and Company, The Riverside Press, 1895) 187.

'And to watch you sink by the fireside now
Back again, as you mutely sit
Musing by fire-light, that great brow
and the spirit-small hand proping it,
Yonder, my heart knows how!

[165] The king speaks about the Holy Land, in "King Henry IV," Part I, Act I. William Shakespeare, *The Complete Works of William Shakespeare* 12 (Boston: The Jefferson Press): 4.

[166] This would have been the answer of faith Phillip failed to give.

* Ecclesiastes 9:10.

with thee.' These omissions of ours which occur in the course of conversation are not unnoted. Philip had a golden opportunity, and he lost it.[168]

(v. 7) 'Two hundred pennyworth.' His view was the sordid one, which too many of us entertain—that want of money is an insuperable difficulty to any great act of generous service; and we are content to do nothing and sigh 'Oh, if one were rich, what a lot of good one could do!' Philip's is the sort of non-committal answer that most of us would have given on such an occasion.

(v. 8) 'Andrew... saith unto Him.' Andrew is more ready for a venture of faith. He is 'Simon Peter's brother,' and it was Simon Peter who made the great confession—'Thou art the Christ.' Andrew, too, sees great possibilities; had not the master raised the dead and healed the sick and gladdened the heart of the wedding guests? Here was a lad with five barley loaves and two (small) fishes; enough to make a meal for one man, anyway; might not Jesus do something with these? But he is afraid of his own temerity; he has gone too far, committed himself to an impossibility, an absurdity even, and hastens to add with due caution—'but what are these among so many?'

(v. 10) 'Make the people sit down.' This story, in all its details, is dear to us as an exquisite revelation of the mind of Christ,—the orderly sitting-down to a meal; the sitting in rows, open squares or oblong figures of even numbers, a hundred at each side and fifty across, probably twenty of such figures forming a circle around Christ and His disciples; the picturesque effect which caught the eye of the evangelist; 'much grass in the place;' the expectant silence of the seated multitude as they regarded absurdly small provision placed before them, —we see it all and love to think of our Lord standing in the midst dealing out bread to that

---

[168] Mason gives here an exhortation to speak regularly on the basis of faith, not dwelling primarily upon the difficulties.

multitude, as indeed he deals it out to us.[169]

(v. 11) 'Having given thanks.' Our grace before meals would be less a formality with us if we remembered its origin.[170] We ponder the story and wonder at what point the miracle of the increase took place. The key to this miracle, as to that of the general resurrection, is to be found in the last chapter (v. 25).[171] 'He gave to the Son also to have life in Himself.'[172] Organic life can be sustained only upon organic life. If we feed upon that which is decayed we perish;[173] and, as we have been told, that secret of life, which our scientist have been unable to track home, lies in Christ— 'in Him was life.'[174] As for how, by what detailed process, the miracle took place, we know no more than we know how an ear of corn is built up, 'first the blade, then the ear, then the full corn in the ear.'[175]

'Distributed.' We read in the other gospels that Christ distributed to the disciples who in turn distributed to the people. So is it still, not immediately but mediately does He deal out to each of us our portions of good things of life:—He 'uses us to help

---

[169] Mason remarks how ordered space is a necessary condition for the provision of food in a shared meal. Here it is suggested that these are conditions for effective teaching. There is a direct connection between the feeding of the multitude and Jesus feeding our spiritual needs.

[170] Thanksgiving before meals follows the example of Christ. Mason always opposes 'formalism' i.e. the practice of ritual without dwelling upon its spiritual meaning.

[171] And there are also many other things which Jesus did, the which, if they should be written every one, I suppose that even the world itself could not contain the books that should be written. Amen. John 21:25.

[172] For as the Father hath life in himself; so hath he given to the Son to have life in himself; John 5:26.

[173] Spiritual feeding upon Christ is a necessary feeding for spiritual life.

[174] In him was life; and the life was the light of men. John 1:4.

* Mark 4:28.

each other so.'[176]

(v. 12) 'Gather up the broken pieces.' Here is another illustration of the beautiful mind of Christ. Where there is all power and all riches there is no waste, but that care of material which belongs to those who know and realise how much is involved in the production of that which we call common.

(v. 14) 'This is of a truth the prophet.' The people were right. He who feeds us as a bird feeds her young ('open thy mouth wide and I will fill it'),[177] supplies the manifold hunger of our manifold nature, He is the Prophet that cometh into the world.

N.B.—Will subscribers who have not paid for this term's *Meditations* kindly send 1/- to Mr. George Middleton, Ambleside, *without delay.*

---

[176] Robert Browning "Fra Lippo Lippi," in Curtis Hidden Page, *British Poets of the Nineteenth Century: Poems by Wordsworth, Coleridge* (Boston: Benj. H. Sanborn & Co. 1910) 648.

> ... Art was given for that:
> God uses us to help each other so.
> Lending our minds out. Have you notice now...

[177] I am the LORD thy God, which brought thee out of the land of Egypt: open thy mouth wide, and I will fill it. Psalms 81:10.

SCALE HOW 'MEDITATIONS'

Dominus Illuminatio Mea

No. 20

FOURTH SUNDAY AFTER TRINITY

Christ our 'Providence'
(S. John 6:15-22)[178]
PART II

(v. 15) 'Jesus therefore perceiving,' etc. The multitude followed the common instinct of men. The 'loaf' giver has ever been the lord or lady, the queen or the king. May we venture to think that our Lord withdrew Himself into the mountain alone to pray, as we are told in S. Mark, against another temptation of the devil? Anyway, this forcing of kingship upon Him was exactly on the lines of the early temptation—'all the kingdoms of the world and the glory of them.' Since then, two years of incessant labour—labour of the most depressing kind, the continual forcing of a higher ideal upon unwilling souls[179]—had intervened and His kingdom had not come. Even of the disciples it is said at this period, 'they understood not concerning the loaves, for their heart was hardened.'[180] What wonder if, when men declined to enter into that kingdom of God which he came to establish, the Saviour should for a moment be tempted by the possibility of a temporal kingship

---

[178] Mason, *The Parents' Review* 20, no. 1 (January 1909): 62-65.

[179] Mason points out that the harder labor is that of holding ideals before those who are not interested.

* S. Mark 6:52.

for the opportunities it would give of bestowing those 'gifts for men,' which men would not receive at His hands. But Jesus withdrew Himself, took time to be alone, took time to pray, and the moment of temptation passed. Here we have an example for our guidance in those moments of popularity when we receive glory one of another. Let us withdraw for a time, let us be alone, let us pray.[181]

(v. 16, 17) The picture is familiar and dear—the sudden squall, as on our own mountain lakes, the disciples rowing for hours and making no headway, Christ watching them from the mountain—we might even imagine with his hand shading His eyes, —he sees their distress and their confusion is increased by the sudden darkness of the East. The fact that Jesus had not yet come to them increased their perplexity; possibly they expected Him to take another boat and join them.

(v. 18) 'The sea was rising by reason of the great wind that blew,'—a tempest, on a confined mountain lake, more full of risk than on the open sea.

(v. 19) 'They had rowed,' etc. They had managed to make between three or four miles and were perhaps in mid sea when, out of the darkness, moving across the uneasy waters, they saw what at first filled them with affright. An apparition, they thought, not the less to be feared because it was the 'ghost' of the Master. Was it He, or was it an evil spirit in His form, one of those demons which the superstitious mind has ever associated with darkness and tempest?

(v. 20) Jesus sees their terror, and through all sounds of the tempest they hear the accents they had learned to love—'It is I, be not afraid!'

(v. 21) 'They were willing.' They had been fearful and most

---

[181] Prayer and solitude are recommended as a means to face the temptation of seeking earthly glory.

unwilling that what they regarded as a spectre should come into their midst. They could bear the worst that the storm could do to them, even to shipwreck and death, but this added terror of the supernatural was too awful to be endured. But they hear the voice of the Son of man, their hearts turn to him and they are *willing*.[182] However strange the scene, however awful His progress over the unstable waters, it is enough for them to know that it is he; they are willing to receive Him into the boat. 'and straight way the boat was at the land.' S. Mark tells us that the wind ceased, the wary leagues of troubled sea stretch no longer before them, straight way, immediately, they are at the haven where they would be.

We know well that this is more than a miracle. It is a parable, a type of how the Master deals with us, His disciples, in the times of our darkness and distress, when we are nigh swallowed by the 'waves of this troublesome world.'[183] We labour to right ourselves, to bale out the waters, to make headway by the strength of our own arms; a darkness falls, we are desolate, alone, exhausted, hopeless of any salvation from the overwhelming waters of temporal or spiritual terrors overwhelm us. Are the powers of darkness in league against us or are we in the hands of an angry God? And then, when we are at our extremity of grief or dismay, those divine accents fall on our ear. All of us perhaps, the evil and the good, have heard them at some time in our lives. In some hour of peril or desolation, the 'It is I' of Christ has come home to us: we have been brought face to face with our Lord. We know that it is He who is dealing with us, in His love and in His pity; no spirit of evil and no offended God. We become *willing* in this day of His power[184] and receive him into the sorely-tossed bark of our lives,

---

[182] Here is another instance where Mason remarks the importance of "willing", this as a response to the disciples perception that it was Jesus coming to them not a specter.

[183] Christina Georgina Rossetti, "The Waves of this Troublesome World, A Tale of Hastings Fifteen Years Ago." *Commonplace, and other Short Stories* (London: FS Ellis, 1870) 269.

and then we learn that all this has come upon us to give Him the opportunity to make Himself know as our Saviour and our Friend. For the distress vanishes, the troublous circumstances smooth themselves out, the end which we has been labouring for, and which seems so very far away, suddenly arrives. With Christ in the boat all is well with us. We realise for an instant the meaning of the Church of Christ when we catch a fleeting glimpse of the millions of troubled souls who through the ages have subsided into happy calm at the words, 'It is I, be not afraid?' 'in all time of our tribulation... Good Lord Deliver us.'[185]

But what for the person whose intellectual convictions will not allow him to receive the notion of a miracle, of any action contrary to the 'laws of nature.' Ichabod![186] He cries. The joy and comfort of this most blessed of the gospel stories has departed for him—that a living, breathing, a man should walk upon the unstable waters, that a word should assuage the storm—these things are to him simply *impossible.* 'Miracles do not happen' is his verdict. The contention is the old one. Has Spirit power over matter? Does the Spirit of God move over the face of the waters? Is there, in fact, any Spirit? There is no answer in the circle of facts to these questions. We cannot know unless we are willing to be raised to that higher plane of thought where the things of the Spirit are discerned.[187] There is nothing to be said to those who frankly

---

[184] Thy people shall be willing in the day of thy power, in the beauties of holiness from the womb of the morning: thou hast the dew of thy youth. Psalms 110:3.

[185] Mason relates the personal experience of the disciple with the collective experience of the whole church universal and finishes with a quotation from the Litany which is part of the prayers of the Anglican Book of Common Prayer.

[186] Lit. Hebrew world meaning 'inglorious,' 'And she named the child Ichabod, saying, The glory is departed from Israel: because the ark of God was taken, and because of her father in law and her husband.' 1 Samuel 4:21.

[187] Mason answers the problem of doubt with the notion that faith allows entrance into a higher plane for reason which provides meaning to existence. The

disavow, with the Sadducees, the Resurrection, angels, spirits and any such thing; but for those, who still hold their faith in God and who are yet quelled and discomforted by allusions to the 'laws of nature,' it is worth while to consider whether they are not occupying a quite untenable position. There is no middle way between absolute faith in God which is able to receive any miracle consistent with the divine character and further unfolding this character to us, and the standpoint of the materialist to whom miracle, prayer, and spirit are alike meaningless.[188] The very phrase 'laws of nature,' convenient and necessary as it is to the scientific student, lands us in an unexpected region of thought when it is used in a final sense. For if Nature have laws which she has presumably originated, if these be the only laws we know and obey, then is Nature sentient and we are in danger of reviving, under the august name of science the Nature worship of more primitive races.[189]

N.B.—There are still several defaulters! Subscriptions for next term should be paid by October 1st, and the 'Meditation' can only be sent to those whose subscriptions are prepaid.

---

answer to such questions will never be found within the limits of sensible perception, or materialism.

[188] Mason rejects agnosticism as an untenable position.

[189] The concept of the 'laws of nature' apart from the Law Giver, idolizes nature as a god. Mason rejects hylozoism.

No. 21

CHRIST, THE BREAD OF LIFE I

(*S. John 6:22-28*)[190]

We have already considered our Lord in the light of our Providence in destitution and in danger; and by this teaching the Evangelist has prepared the way for a broader, fuller, revelation. The instinct of the human soul who is beginning to know our Lord is to seek Him in emergencies of danger and of necessity, and the most comforting stories of the feeding of the five thousand and the stilling of the tempest bring us the assurance that no cry 'out of the depths'[191] will fail to reach His ear and enlist His help. But the Evangelist is about to unfold a fuller teaching: he will show us Christ not only as our Saviour in our great occasions, but as the sole and continuous Sustenance of man.[192]

(v. 22) 'On the morrow,' etc., *i.e.*, the morrow after the teaching and feeding of the five thousand, the night of which had been spent in peril of storm by the disciples on the lake. 'The multitude': He himself, we are told, sent the multitude away,[193] but either they had returned to the scene of the miracle or had returned to Bethsaida, on the other side of the Sea of Galilee, the scene of the miracle. They are perplexed, apparently, for they had seen how Jesus sent His disciples away in the only boat there, and had not entered it Himself, and yet He was not to be found.

---

[190] Mason, "Christ the Bread of Life" *The Parents' Review* 20, no. 2 (February 1909): 138-142.

[191] 'Out of the depths have I cried unto thee, O LORD.' Psalms 130:1.

[192] Mason upholds the doctrine of the Uniqueness of Christ: 'The Sole, and continuous sustenance of man.'

* Mark 6:45.

(v. 23) Meantime other boats had come from Tiberias, drawn thither, no doubt, by reports of the wonder which had been performed. 'After the Lord had given thanks.' It is interesting to observe that this is the single note of the miracle which the Evangelist thinks it well to preserve. Plainly the giving of thanks did not seem to him formal or accidental, but as the essential feature of the miracle; that is, he saw that in this, as in all things, Christ was in continual co-operation with the Father, and more, was in continual appreciation of, and gratitude for, the Father's intervention. It is worth while to ask ourselves why Christ gave thanks. The simple and obvious answer, because he felt thankful, will perhaps make our hearts condemn us as among the unthankful and the evil who do not inherit the Kingdom of God.[194] Even though 'thank God' arise in our hearts spontaneously a hundred times a day, we still feel that our recognition lags behind the continual mercies of our God. Perhaps after our study of this discourse at Capernaum we may realise a little more the meaning of 'life' and the meaning of ' bread,' and that 'grace before meat,' which is apt to be a mocking formality, may become to us very full of meaning and very full of praise. All our happiness, whether in a bright day, or a true friend, or joyous work, must have its complementary expression—the 'thank God' ever burning as a duly trimmed lamp in our hearts. But we act as spoiled children, unthankful less from want of heart than from want of thought. Let us pull ourselves up and consider, and not fail in that responsive thankfulness which is the recognition of the Giver behind the gift.

(v. 24) So, after a vain search for Jesus and His disciples, 'they themselves got into the boats from Tiberias and came to Capernaum.' Already known as our Lord's own city, 'seeking Jesus.'

(v. 25) They find the Master, and there is in their question the

---

[194] Men shall be lovers of their own selves, covetous, boasters, proud, blasphemers, disobedient to parents, unthankful, unholy, 2 Tim. 3:2.

sort of petulent reproach which a crowd will feel itself at liberty to bestow on the favourite of the hour: 'Rabbi, when camest Thou hither?'

(v. 26) 'Jesus answered.' Another of those marvellous answers, which are no reply to the words which have been spoken, but are a sudden unveiling as by a search-light of the thoughts of the hearts of the speakers. Christ knew that they had been seeking Him and He shows them why—'not because ye saw signs, but because ye ate of the loaves.' Once again, does not our heart condemn us? We, too, seek Christ, not because we see signs of things ineffable in the daily occurrences and surroundings of our lives, but because we have eaten of the loaves—of His comfort and help and satisfaction hitherto—and we have present needs which we bring before him. But we need not reproach ourselves: this, too, is right and belongs to the prayer which He taught us—'give us this day our daily bread,' and thereby give us satisfaction for every need of body, soul, and spirit. It is the part of Children to go to their father on all their occasions and in all their distresses. The multitude had not done amiss, and because they had done thus much our Lord judges them ready to learn of the greater and deeper things which were yet to be done. They had seen the sign, but had not understood the thing signified. The sign itself was a sufficiently good thing for them: just as all the bread of comfort and water of refreshment which we find on our way is apt to be enough for us. We do not look deeper and ask, what does it all mean?

(v. 27) Eastern sages and Western philosophers alike have ever reserved their deepest esoteric teachings for the inner few, the chosen disciples who have followed them through the labyrinth of their teaching. Not so does Christ. He offers to a multitude, with no characteristic except that they sought Him,—and sought Him as He Himself declares, for a less worthy reason,—teaching which penetrates beyond the things seen and temporal to the things unseen and eternal. They are to 'work not for the meat which perisheth, but for the meat which abideth unto eternal life.' This unlearned multitude is brought face to face with the two great problems of our being—What is life? And, What is meat? And very fit is that these questions should be brought before the multitude, for every man born into the world finds some solution which satisfies himself, and upon his answers depends the manner of man he is and will become. The answer of Christ was found a 'hard saying,' not only by the multitude, but by many of His disciples. It is still found a hard saying, and divides not only the world but the Church into two camps—those who can and those who cannot receive it. The meaning to us of the blessed Sacrament, the sign and, so far as it is truly the sign, the vehicle of that substance which is the life, depends upon our apprehension of Life and Meat.[195] And because we will not fully understand, this Sacrament of peace has been to the Church the standard round which perpetual contention has raged.[196] The answer of Christ may be 'hard,' but though philosophers and men of science have sought from the beginning into the sources of meaning of the mystery of life, no other answer has been found. Our Lord has spoken the last word. He is the Life and He is the Bread. What, then of the endless forms which life assumes, from the hyssop that groweth upon the wall to the cedar of Lebanon, from the insect flitting in the summer sun to the ox upon whose flesh human life is nourished? The developments are many and individual, but the principle of life is one; the scientific and the ignorant agree in this; all recognize a quality in all living things to which they can give no name but that of life; for which they can

---

[195] This is the key to Mason's sacramental understanding of existence. Jesus is the life and the bread. Life sustains life. The principle of life is one. All life is a manifestation of the life of God. 'The Bread is made of the living seed.' 'The wine is crushed from the living fruit'. Food nourishes, because it is living. The Word of Christ feeds the soul of man.

[196] Mason takes the classical Anglican position that the worthy recipient feeds spiritually upon the true food of life which is Christ.

discern no cause; for which principle they are able to discern that disease and decay are only a means of liberation. Our carnal and material minds are willing to receive it that all life is derived from God, as a gift is derived from a giver, but we shrink from the thought that all life is a manifestation of the very life of God.[197] Perhaps we shall approach to some realisation of the meaning of the mystery of those outward and visible signs—the bread which is made from the *living* seed, the wine which is crushed from the *living* fruit—when we perceive why these things sustain even our bodily life. All the life that we have, of whatever sort, is the life of Christ, and in proportion as we realise that which is least, we shall perceive, however dimly, that which is greatest, and every eating of bread and drinking of wine will become to us, in a lesser degree, sacramental. But life, like the tabernacle in the wilderness, has its three courts. There is the outer court where living things blossom and bear fruit, eat and drink, and sleep and play; and this life is holy, and disease and fever do not extinguish, but liberate, the principle of life. There is the Holy place where not all living beings walk but only mankind, because men are able to think and love; this life also is sustained upon Christ, who is our life. Within, there is the Holy of Holies, where man communicates with God and consciously receives in Christ the life of his spirit.[198]

---

[197] This is the key to Mason's sacramental understanding of reality. 'All living things are a manifestation of the very life of God.'

[198] Every meal is sacramental. Food conveys the principle of life common to all. This sacramental understanding is the key to Mason's ontology. Every aspect of life is consecrated. The life of thought is the common life of knowledge given to human kind. The highest level of life is communion with Christ, the life. In the Holy Communion by faith, the highest aim of existence is given: Life eternal and the knowledge of God.

SCALE HOW 'MEDITATIONS'
Dominus Illuminatio Mea

No. 22

EIGTEENTH SUNDAY AFTER TRINITY
(S. John 6:27-35)

'THE BREAD OF GOD' [199]

(v. 27) 'For Him the Father, even God, hath sealed,' that is, set apart for peculiar office as a sovereign is set apart when he is anointed. The Son of man reveals Himself as set apart to be the continual Sustainer of mankind.[200] What a thought of comfort in every time of famine that comes upon us—body, heart, or spirit—to know that there is a Sustainer standing by holding in His hands, offering for our acceptance, that very meat which we require at the moment.

(v. 28) 'What must we do,' etc. The multitude is responding to the teaching of Christ. A *sincere* request for direction is a sign of grace, and that their question was sincere we know, because the first stirrings of grace in all our hearts lead us to the same enquiry. We perceive that there is a work of God to be done, and to be done by us, and we ask eagerly what it is,—

'that we may go and do it straight away.'

We ask faithfully it is true, but we do not always keep silence

---

[199] Charlotte Mason, "The Bread of God" *The Parents' Review* 20, no. 2 (February 1909): 142-146.

[200] The Son as sustainer complements the notion of Holy Spirit as the educator of mankind.

in our hearts waiting for the reply of our Lord. We answer our own question according to our own inclinations. We rush into one kind of good work or another, and our work is not service, because it is spoiled by wilfulness. Even when we abide in that vocation to which we are called we find ways to spoil our work by that wilfulness which appears to us to be zeal. Then, health fails or spirits flag; we weary of our self-chosen labour, and especially do we weary of the people we have been trying to help or to serve. We say, 'What's the good?' 'It's no use trying.' The poor are 'ungrateful,' our own belongings do not 'understand' or 'appreciate.' For a time at any rate the works of God are not for us, and we settle down to go our own way until the Divine Voice shall appeal to us once again.

(v. 29) 'Jesus answered.' Here we have our Lord's recognition of the sincerity of the speakers; His answer to the thoughts of their hearts is also an answer to the words they have spoken. He tells them and us, for all time, what is the work of God. They have spoken of 'works' manifold. Christ replies that for all men, every where, there is but one work of God. They had spoken of *doing*; Christ replies that his one work of God does not consist in *doing*, but in *believing*—'that ye believe on Him whom He hath sent.' In other words, the thing that matters in the sight of God (and indeed in that of men also) is not what we do, but the attitude of our minds in doing it. It is not easy to see at first how believing on Christ is indeed working the works of God. But let us consider for a moment what we mean by believing in a person. Such faith is an act of recognition, born of close attention for hours, or months, or years. We have considered the ways of this person in whom we believe, and by the intuition of sympathy have apprehended his motives. We *know* him; we recognise him, and our faith cannot be shaken. That which we admire we must needs imitate and we mould ourselves on the pattern of the person in whom we believe.[201]

---

[201] Imitation is the fruit of meditation, faith produces action in kind.

This is believing on the ordinary human level. To believe in Christ is this, with an added element which makes the transforming power complete. First we think upon Him; we dwell upon every circumstance of His life, every word of His teaching; we keep Him in all our thoughts.[202] We eat and drink, not only at the blessed Sacrament, but all times, 'in remembrance of Him.'[203] We begin to see that He lived all His years to lose His life, not once at the end, but all the time, and

'sore paineth
Us this continual Dying that constraineth.'

The world is to us a place in which to have and to hold the things of the mind, of the heart, or the world; but *His* outstretched hands grasped not any treasure. We choose to be free and independent, to go where we list, to do what we like; *His* feet, nailed to the cross, moved not on His pleasure. We love to rule, to have our own way, to be of importance; Christ said, 'I am among you as he that serveth.' We choose to be independent, to have our own way; Christ claims to act always as one 'sent.' As we meditate upon Christ, as we learn to believe on him, to realise that all blessedness lies in sacrifice and service, in lowliness and meekness, we begin to understand how great is the conversion that must take place in us if we are ever to have in us the mind that was in Christ Jesus.[204] We become irritated and impatient; we find it unnatural and impossible to take his Life for our pattern.

---

[202] This explains the central place meditation upon the life of Christ has for Mason's educational philosophy. Its founding stone is: knowing Jesus Christ personally. Masons educational theory and practice is a philosophy of discipleship.

[203] Every meal becomes a sacred opportunity bearing sacramental importance.

[204] Meditation upon Christ lies at the root of conversion, discipleship and education.

(v. 30) So the multitude. 'What then doest Thou for a sign that we may see and believe?' This was not what they wanted—a Person who should fulfil all righteousness before their eyes, and lift them out of the unrighteousness and selfishness which was easy and pleasant into that sore and difficult beauty of holiness which was his. No, but they would be as the birds of the air who find a table ever spread. They would feed on continual manna; they would have what they wanted, whatever good things their souls desired. That and that only was the use of a Lord to them. Had they not had a sign? Had not five thousand of them eaten and been filled of what should have been a scanty meal for two or three? Yes, and therefore they perceived the power in Christ to be another Moses to them, and to give them from day to day the bread without labour for which they clamoured. Before we condemn this careless multitude, let us ask ourselves whether our own demands of our Lord are in any way like theirs. Do we come to Him chiefly for meat that perisheth?

(v. 32) 'It was not Moses that gave you the bread.' Our Lord is not wearied with the wilfulness of the people. In answer to their querulous demand He reveals the origin of all that nourishes men in body, soul, and spirit.[205] The poem who fires us with high thoughts, the inventor who makes the ways of life easy, the farmer who produces bread—it is not Moses nor another; not any of these from whom we get the food that quickens us—they are but the vehicles.

(v. 33) 'The bread of God' is one, however it be conveyed, and is to be known by two signs:— It cometh down out of heaven and is holy, heavenly, undefiled; and it giveth life unto the world. The life-giving thought or discovery, the food and the teaching by which men live, are all of Him.[206]

---

[205] These categories correspond with the three levels of life, mentioned above in the image of the tabernacle: natural life, intellectual life, spiritual life.

[206] The unity of truth and life in Christ is made the foundation of all

(v. 34) Again we see ourselves in the crowd; when we think of these things our hearts burnt within us; we, too, would cry with them, 'Lord, evermore give us this bread,' howsoever poor and material was their conception of the bread they asked for.

(v. 35) Again our Lord responds to a sincere prayer, if a shallow one. He reveals to their slow hearts the central truth of all our living—'I am the Bread of Life: he that cometh to Me shall not hunger, and he that believeth on Me shall never thirst.' We all know something of the hunger of the heart and the thirst of the soul. We find our cup of life poor and unsatisfying; we want to know and to have and to do great things. We are sick of the trivial round, the common task,[207] weary of the people about us, weary of ourselves, bored, dissatisfied, discontented; we do not know what is the matter with us, but all the time we are fainting for hunger, famishing for thirst. We seek for satisfaction at many sources. We ask, above all things, to be amused, constantly amused, so that there may be no time for our thoughts to turn back upon themselves. We would have love, lawful or unlawful; excitement, passion, the lusts of the flesh—anything to deliver us from the sameness of every day. Knowledge, too, we would have above that which is written, whether from the 'Mahatma' or the 'Medium'; but in none of these things do we find rest.[208] People go about with the lines of weariness and discontent engraved upon their faces, for how can a hungry man feel satisfied, and how can one be content unless he is satisfied? The 'unrest of the age,' what

---

education as a means to nourish life with the life coming from God, 'the food and the teaching by which men live, are all of Him.

[207] John Keble, *The Christian Year,* 3.

> 'The trivial round, the common task,
> Would furnish all we ought to ask;
> Room to deny ourselves; a road
> To bring us daily nearer God.'

[208] Mason rejects the tyranny of amusement and spiritual speculation beyond that which is written in Scripture. Only Christ can satisfy man's hunger.

is it but the hunger of the heart and the thirst of the soul, to be satisfied alone by Him who is the sole sustenance provided for men? 'He that cometh to Me shall never hunger, and he that believeth on Me shall never thirst.' There are people who are dissatisfied with the present and hopeless for the future—pessimists they are called—and there are other who have glo☐rious optimistic dreams for the future but expect nothing from the present. There are, too, those to whom the present, incomplete as it is, yields full content and satisfaction; because they are they for whom it is written that they shall neither hunger nor thirst; they to whom the final Source of satisfaction is ever open.[209]

---

[209] The faithful disciple of Christ Mason was endevouring to foster.

Dominus Illuminatio Mea

No. 23

NINETEENTH SUNDAY AFTER TRINITY
(S. John 5:36-45)

'THE BREAD OF GOD' II [210]

(v. 36) Our hearts yearn sometimes for the grace granted to these Jews, that we might see with our own eyes Christ in the flesh. 'Seeing is believing,' we say, and we think that a stronger passion of conviction and devotion would have been ours had we been amongst those more favoured who saw Him face to face. But perhaps in the things of Christ seeing is not believing; only those who see beyond the outward and visible, look with the eyes of faith. These Jews saw and yet believed not.

(v. 37) 'All that which the Father giveth me shall come.' Here we are brought face to face with that doctrine of election which, as we understand it, is trying to our sense of justice. Let us be sure when that is the case that we understand amiss; if favouritism is a vice in an earthly ruler, let us boldly say that divine favouritism is impossible. Let us note here that any feeble coming to Christ of which we are aware, any resting on Him in our weariness, any

---

[210] Mason, "The Bread of God, II" *The Parents' Review* 20, no. 3 (March 1909): 216-219.

turning to Him in our distress, is a joyful indication that the Father has had us in His divine counsels and has given us to the Son.[211] Do we fear for the future? Do we tremble lest this should prove a passing phase of feeling? Do we think that we are not worthy to bear the name of Christ? We need not fear—'Him that cometh to Me I will in no wise cast out.'

(v. 38) 'Not to do Mine own will.' We all like to be credited with that work which is especially ours, but our Lord prefers always to take the subordinate place of one carrying out a commission. He tells us nothing of His own goodwill towards us, but speaks only of the will of the Father which brings us to Christ. Here, too may His followers find a key to their lives, and a test of their faithfulness. Do we choose to do what we like; to follow our own inclinations: then are we wilful, and are not following our Master. Do we choose to do or even to suffer the will of our Father:

'holding as creed,
That Circumstance, a sacred oracle,
Speaks with the voice of God to faithful souls' [212]

then are we faithful to Him Who is meek and lowly of heart, and Who came, not to do His own will, but the will of Him that sent Him.

(v.39) 'this is the will,' etc. It is good to rest upon the steadfast faithfulness of our God. The unrest and anxiety which belong to things of this life do not disturb us here; all is safe that has been given into the stewardship of Christ. Observe, it is not said that He will lose no one, but even *no thing*; and *it* shall be raised. We get

---

[211] Mason rejects the interpretation of the doctrine of election as a sign of divine favoritism. This expresses the comfort of the doctrine of predestination for believers as stated in article 17 of the 39 articles of Religion of the Church of England.

[212] Mason, "Moses: A Study" *The Parents' Review* 14, no. 2 (February 1903): 133-134. Also quoted in "Ourselves" *Home Education Series* 4: 117.

here a glimpse of the fullness and richness of the life that shall be.[213]
No heroic impulse, no inspiring thought, no conception of beauty,
no act of service to each other, no single thing instinct with the life
of Christ, shall be lost; but all this 'treasure laid up in Heaven will
go to the fulfilling and enriching of the broader, deeper life':[214] (see
Abt Vogler, concluding stanzas).[215] Nay, may we not hope to find

---

[213] Mason notes that the promise resurrection involves the complete
restoration of everything God will save, from this existence.

[214] 'A broader and deeper life' is a further motive for a rich education, it is a
preparation for eternity in which the perfection of all these good things shall be
enjoyed for ever without limitations.

[215] Robert Browning, *Abt Vogler* 494-495 *English Poetry* (1170-1892).

> Therefore to whom turn I but to thee, the ineffable Name?
> Builder and maker, thou, of houses not made with hands!
> What, have fear of change from thee who art ever the same?
> Doubt that thy power can fill the heart that thy power expands?
> There shall never be one lost good! What was, shall live as before;
> The evil is null, is naught, is silence implying sound;
> What was good shall be good, with, for evil, so much good more;
> On the earth the broken arcs; in the heaven a perfect round.
>
> All we have willed or hoped or dreamed of good shall exist;
> Not its semblance, but itself; no beauty, nor good, nor power
> Whose voice has gone forth, but each survives;
> Are music sent up to God by the lover and the bard;
> Enough that he heard it once: we shall hear it by and by.
> And what is our failure here but a triumph's evidence
> For the fullness of the days? Have we withered or agonized?
> Why else was the pause prolonged but that singing might issue thence?
> Why rushed the discords in, but that harmony should be prized?
> Sorrow is hard to bear, and doubt is slow to clear,
> Each sufferer says his say, his scheme of the weal and woe:
> But God has a few of us whom he whispers in the ear;
> The rest may reason and welcome: 'tis we musicians know.
> Well, it is earth with me; silence resumes her reign:
> I will be patient and proud, and soberly acquiesce.
> Give me the keys. I feel
> for the common chord again,
> Sliding by semitones till I sink to the minor — yes,

again all ready for fulfilling those 'good intentions' which get scant credit here?

'All instincts immature, all purposes unsure,
That weighed not as his work
yet swelled the man's amount.'
(see the whole of *Rabbi Ben Ezra*).[216]

(v. 40) Here we get the resolution of that problem of election which is to many of us a 'hard saying.' Who are those whom the Father gives to the Son? The Father sent the Son, we know, to be the Saviour of the World; it is the divine will that all should believe; but here we see where the election comes in. It is we who choose. 'For this is the will of My Father that every one that beholdeth the Son.' Here our Lord describes, by the use of another verb, that act of fixed attention of the soul by which we recognise and apprehend Christ, that act of meditating, thinking upon Him, which our Lord requires of us in the blessed Sacrament—'This do in *remembrance* of me.'[217] 'And believeth';—our Lord here indicates the two stages of the act of faith; first the fixed, humble, and open-minded attention; and next the sure and satisfying conviction which comes of beholding Christ;[218] and this is eternal life, because it is 'to know the Father and Jesus Christ Whom He hath sent.'

And I blunt it into a ninth, and I stand on alien ground,
Surveying awhile the heights I rolled from into the deep;
Which, hark, I have dared and done, for my resting-place is found,
The C Major of this life: so, now I will try to sleep.

[216] Robert Browning, "Rabbi Ben Ezra". In light of the importance of this reference to elucidate Mason's views concerning the afterlife I have included the whole poem as an Appendix, see page 251.

[217] Again Mason stresses meditation, beholding Christ is the key to the Christian life, and relates it with the teaching of the Eucharist as a solution to the problem of election. The Father gives to the Son all who behold and believe Christ.

[218] Faith has two stages, humble attention, and conviction.

'And I will raise him up at the last day.' It is as if Christ felt the pulse of His audience, the sceptical thought rising in the hearts of even the faithful—'All men die; what is this about eternal life?' Christ's answer is again the promise of the joyful resurrection.

(v. 41) 'The Jews therefore murmured, etc. 'The Jews,' *par excellence*,[219] does not imply the nation as a whole but those of the Jews, Scribes, and Pharisees, whose lives were devoted to the keeping of the ceremonial law, with its infinitesimal and never ceasing observances. By their superior 'sanctity' these men had obtained a hold over the people and, wherever Christ taught, there were they, probably hanging on the outskirts of the crowd, waiting, not to learn, not to receive and believe, but to criticise and condemn, to do what our Lord describes as 'murmuring.' They are evidently men of trained minds; they know how to lay their finger on the salient point of the discourse. They raise no question about the gift of eternal life, nor even about the resurrection. What offends them is, that Christ should give Himself out to be sustenance of His people; their present life and therefore their life eternal, that divine 'meat' which came down from heaven.

(v. 42) 'And they said, Is not this Jesus the son of Joseph.' Here we have an epitome of all destructive criticism. It is quite conclusive, 'whose father and mother we know,' and yet it does not touch the point; the Christ who laboured to reveal Himself to these slow of heart in His intimate relation with every one of them was not to be known in the flesh. His earthly home and up-bringing had nothing to do with the matter; they conceived that they knew all when they knew nothing. The spiritual descendants of these Jews are active to-day. They credit Christ with a just life, even claim Him as their highest example, but that He 'came down from heaven?'—no; are not all the conditions of His life as a man among men fully known? Why entertain the superstitious and idolatrous

---

[219] Text changed to: "in this connection" on *The Parent's Review* edition of this Meditation.

notion that a man among other men should be as God? So they continue to murmur among themselves; keen of insight after their kind, but blind to all those things of the Spirit which are spiritually discerned. Where this destructive criticism does not consciously touch the Son of God, it is all the same in our midst. We all live in houses made with hands, but about us, wherever we are, in the family or in our vocation, is also a house not made with hands. We can take this house to pieces stone by stone, and as we pull it down look at each stone and say—'this is no house, no home, for my soul,' or we can abide where we are called to be, in our special sphere, in our Church in our country,[220] and say with Jacob 'surely the Lord is in this place and I knew it not.'[221]

(v. 43) 'Murmur not among yourselves.' Here is a counsel for our lives, too; it is not by the murmurings of destructive criticism that wrongs are remedied, failings corrected, or truth discerned.

'No man can come,' etc. Our Lord reiterates what He has said before, as His custom is: but in each repetition a further truth is revealed. The divine Father Himself draws the willing soul to the divine Son: our hearts bow down in reverence before the tenderness and beauty of this thought: may He awaken our ear to hear and our hearts to respond to the secret drawings of the divine Word.

'And I will raise him up at the last day.' The third assurance of the joyful resurrection given on this one occasion as if for strongest confirmation.

(v. 45) 'And they shall all be taught of God.'[222] Our Lord reveals what this teaching shall be; they shall be taught to see God manifest in the flesh in the face of Jesus Christ. 'Everyone that

---

[220] Church and country are identified as the proper place for the exercise of our vocation in our particular sphere of influence.

* Genesis 28:16.

* See Isaiah 54:13.

hath heard from the Father.' 'Hear from'—delightful, familiar, phrase, that we use of letters from absent friends. Just so, does not one hear from the Father in the written letter of His Word, in the inner whisperings of His Spirit? And always the message is one; everyone who 'hath heard,' says our Lord, and 'hath learned' cometh unto Me.

Dominus Illuminatio Mea

No. 24

TWENTIETH SUNDAY AFTER TRINITY
(S. John 6:45-60)[223]

(v. 45) Our Lord had disclosed the secret of His kingdom—that only those came to Him who had received into their hearts communications from the Father.

(v. 46) Now the good Shepherd, as ever, goes in advance of His sheep to forfend them from the dangers of the way. He who has 'hear from the Father' may easily figure to himself that he has seen the Father, and so superstitious imaginations and idolatrous images might creep into the worship of Him who must be worshipped in spirit and in truth; there is no vision of the Father for men only in Christ,[224] 'He which is from God, he hath seen the Father.'

(v. 47 and 48) Through these repeated asseverations we seem to hear, not only our Lord's solemn witness to the truth and vital importance of His statements, but also an undertone of sadness and protest that words so full of blessing for men must be repeated again and again, and yet they will not understand nor receive. So it is still: we seek 'life' in many quests of pleasure or of gain; we will not open our minds to the healing thought that he that believeth hath already that fulfilment of desire which is

[223] Mason, "The Bread of God, III" *The Parents' Review* 20, no. 3 (March 1909): 220-224.

[224] Christ alone.

eternal life, that satisfaction of his soul's hunger which the 'bread of life' alone gives.

(v. 49) 'Your father did eat the manna,' etc. Our Lord again returns to the opening thought of His discourse—the comparison raised by the people between the perennial manna and the fugitive meal which He had provided for them. In the bread they have eaten at His hands, as in the manna which 'Moses' gave them, they are to see a figure of which He Himself, standing before them, is the fulfilment. These things showed forth Christ, but with a difference; the manna came as a table of the Lord spread daily for the people, it is true, but the people who had eaten of it died.

(v. 50) 'this is the bread,' etc. And then the King repeats the royal offer of bread, bread enough and to spare for every man, that a man may eat thereof and not die.'

(v. 51) 'I am the living bread,' etc. Our Lord stands before the people in that synagogue at Capernaum, a living breathing Man, and again repeats that amazing saying—that he Himself is the 'living bread,' the sustenance of the world, come down out of heaven; that, if any man, whosoever he be, eat of this bread, a principle of life[225] shall be awakened within him, a fullness of life and joy which can never be extinguished; he shall live for ever.

Yet, 'and the bread which I will give is My flesh;' here we have the note of sacrifice familiar to the Jewish people—flesh given, offered in sacrifice, consumed upon the altar—they knew very well what that meant, but not the application of it. How could this man give His flesh in sacrifice and His body as food 'for the life of the *world*'? Here is a note that would not strike pleasantly upon Jewish ears; for were *they* not the peculiar people? There was so much else perplexing in this strange discourse that they allowed this saying to pass, but very probably it rankled and swelled the sum of their account against Christ.

---

[225] Jesus, the sustenance of life, is the principle of life, eternal life.

(v. 52) 'The Jews therefore strove one with another saying,' etc. Now wonder that they 'strove.' Such utterances from one in their midst must, we should think, either come home to them with heart-piercing conviction or excite their fierce scorn and indignation. But, standing before Christ, they cannot put His words away from them; a side-issue presents itself—'How can this man give us his flesh to eat?' Here we have an epitome of the controversy which has raged in the Church for many centuries, and is raging hotly as ever to-day. In this discourse of the bread of life our Lord sets forth the general principle that he is the sustenance of His people, that, whenever they manifest life, in whatever direction, that life, that power and joy, is immediately derived from Him. S. John does not tell us of the institution of that Sacrament of the body and blood of Christ whereto His people are required to come on set occasions, that they may be especially and peculiarly sustained; but the twelve who were present when—'Jesus took bread and blessed and brake it; and he gave to the disciples and said, Take, eat, this is My body'—must have recognised in those words a summing up of the discourse which had in earlier days tested their faith. The teaching at the Last Supper, with its outward and visible signs, is the summing up and embodiment of this unfolding to men of the means whereby they live.[226] Like these Jews, the Christian Church has never argued that it was impossible that Christ should so sustain His people, but sections of the church have ever striven among themselves as to *how* this thing should be? Is the sacrament of the Lord's body merely a sign of things spiritual or does it in itself convey spiritual sustenance? Is the sustenance actually contained in the elements in some spiritual and indistinguisha□ble form? Or is it, as the elements are received by the faithful that they convey divine sustenance? Or is it, indeed, that their very substance is changed

---

[226] The sacrament of the Holy Communion therefore subsumes Mason's views concerning life, truth, meditation and education. i.e. The Secret of life in Christ.

and they become the true body and blood of Christ?[227] these, and such as these, are the burning questions that have ever divided the Church; and it is well that we should consider how our Lord answers these Jews in some of whom there would seem to be glimmerings of faith. Our Lord is telling in this discourse, if we may say so reverently, labouring strenuously to tell, all of the truth that can be received. If it is possible for His disciples and the Jews to learn—'*How* can this man give us His flesh to eat'? doubtless he will reveal that also.

(v. 53) The answer vouchsafed by Christ offers no explanation. He does but reiterate solemnly the one principle of life with the addition that 'ye have not life in yourselves' except by this eating and this drinking. It may be that the sustenance of life like the source of life is an ineffable mystery which the heart of man cannot conceive and which therefore cannot be revealed. It may be that our Lord would bid us do our part, the spiritual eating and spiritual drinking,[228] and leave it to him to impart his flesh, which is meat indeed, and His blood, which is drink indeed, how He will. Anyway, all attempts to define where He has not defined would appear to end in controversy and schism, and perhaps we shall not do amiss if we, as members of His church, make it our prayer that the eyes of all Christian people, whether clergy or laity, be turned away from the sore and burning question of *how* the spiritual life is imparted, and be turned towards that most comforting assurance, that, if we will eat we shall be fed, and in feeding upon Christ shall have everlasting life.

(v. 54) 'Except ye eat' was pronounced as a condemnation, and is followed by the renewed promise that 'He that eateth hath eternal life'—expansion, joy, fullness of living here, hardly to be

---

[227] Mason here summarizes the four typical views of the sacrament from memorialism to transubstantiation.

[228] Spiritual drinking and eating is the language of Cranmer and the Anglican Prayer Book.

interrupted by death itself; for, 'I will raise him up at the last day' to the untiring energising uncloyed fulfilment of the perfect life beyond.

(v. 55) 'My flesh is true Meat;' 'My blood is true drink.' We feed ourselves upon dead sea apples, and find them dust and ashes in our mouth. But the true meat which replenishes, which sends us on our way vigorous and rejoicing, the true drink which exhilarates and vitalises our dull frame, this we seek in vain at the sources of knowledge or fame, or of human love even, which is not 'in Christ.'

(v. 56) It would appear as if our Lord could find no words to express too strongly that most intimate tie which exists between him and His believing people who feed upon Him. They abide, not with Him, nor near him, not by him nor beside Him, but in Him, and He abides in them, and this not occasionally—a passing visit—but a continual abiding; an abiding in the full life of Christ as one abides in one's home; not, alas, but that we go in and out, and in the hardness of our hearts forsake at times the life that is ours, but we weary and hurry back as 'doves to their windows,'[229] and are at rest once more in the abiding life.

(v. 57) with one more argument does Christ enforce this supernal teaching—'As I live because of the Father,' that is by means of, so 'he that eateth me shall live' by means of the influx of Life proceeding from me.

(v. 58) 'this is the bread,' etc. Our Lord sums up in these closing words the whole of this great discourse. 'This,' indicating Himself, 'is the bread which came down out of heaven,' and is therefore heavenly, spiritual, not earthly, material. Therefore it is not like the manna of which men eat and died, but 'he that eateth this bread shall live for ever.'

---

* Isaiah 60:8.

(v. 59) 'These things said he in the synagogue.' The remains of the synagogue are still to be seen among the ruins of the Tel Hum, which mark the site of the ancient Capernaum. A stone still exists bearing a carving of the pot of manna preserved in the ark, and this may possibly have served as the text of our Lord's 'object lesson.'

(v. 60) 'This is a hard saying; who can heart it?' We, in our poor measure, are sometimes aware, when we give out the best that is in us, that we have not been understood, and have only succeeded in alienating our hearers. But what is our poor little measure of truth compared with the great revelation which Christ has just made, and what is our disappointment to His, as he sat in the synagogue yearning infinitely over the souls of His hearers? The Jews might well be unprepared; but His own disciples, had they not been led up carefully, step by step, to the very sum and heart of the truth which he has now disclosed to them? will they not receive it joyfully and eat and live?[230] They find it a 'hard saying,' and turn from Him in resentment. This was not what they wanted; they had followed the Messiah, the king of the Jews, whose glory should be open and known to all men; and now what had they instead? This mystic talk of His flesh, and bread, and eternal life, and resurrection,—things for which no man carried any test or measure![231] Surely some of the bitterness of Gethsemane was felt by our Master in that synagogue at Capernaum.

---

[230] 'eating' means receiving the word and living by it.

[231] i.e. a spiritual religion.

SCALE HOW 'MEDITATIONS'

Dominus Illuminatio Mea

No. 25

TWENTY-FIRST SUNDAY AFTER TRINITY
(S. John 6:61-68) [232]

THE DISLOYAL DISCIPLES

(v. 60) 'This is a hard saying.' We have seen that to those disciples who followed Christ with some measure of personal attachment no doubt, but also with an eye to their own advancement in the messianic kingdom, the words of Christ were 'a hard saying.' They had reason—'Have we not thrown up our means of livelihood, given up our homes, our own people, cast everything into this one venture, and now the whole thing turns out to be a delusion, and we are thrown on the world without any prospects at all? We cannot keep a house and spread a table with this manner of meat and drink.' We are grieved for the hardness of their hearts; we think, perhaps, that had we listened we should have better understood. But we who think we understand this word of Christ's, 'I am the Bread of Life,' do we never ask ourselves, *Cui bono?* When we come to some 'hard saying,' when our good is evil spoken of, when our best efforts lack success, when we, too, appear to have left all and followed Christ, and got nothing by it, do we never think to ourselves that it is 'hard;' or are we indeed most able in these times of our hunger and our thirst to come to Christ and eat and drink and be satisfied? If this is not so, if our spirits quail before every adverse wind we had better see to it that we are not among the disloyal disciples who find that special word of Christ to us, which is our life in this world, a 'hard saying.' 'who can hear it?' Who can put up with crosses and losses without any

---

[232] Mason, "The Disloyal Disciples" *The Parents' Review* 20, no. 4 (April 1909): 301-305.

shrinking of faith? there are those who can; and they discover that by these things men live, and that in all such is the life of the Spirit. They discover that that Life, is apt to be most vigorous and active in times of dearth and distress.

The disciples had more excuse than we. They had hardly had time to realise that their leader was their king, nor to ask themselves—What is the one duty which a subject owes to this king? We know that loyalty is our first duty and our last duty, and includes all our duties. Loyalty is the hall-mark of character; and all men are divided into two sorts—the loyal, who are few, but whose lives are beautiful in quietness and confidence; and the disloyal, who are many. All loyalty to each other is loyalty to our Master. Let us be loyal in all our relations, loyal in our words, loyal in even our passing thoughts, and so shall we be loyal in the supreme relation. A precious perfume evaporates from an unstoppered bottle; and loyalty is the jewel and the perfume of the gentle life, which it is our business to keep. How are we to know when it is passing from us?

(v. 61) 'His disciples murmured at this.' The murmuring spirit which finds nothing quite good enough for its deserts in heaven or on earth; not the weather, nor friends, nor circumstances, nor even Almighty God; the spirit which sees the mote in its brother's eye and is blind to the beam in its own eye, this is the spirit that occupies the empty house when the loyal temper has flown. We cannot murmur and be loyal; nor can we take any one bit of our lives apart and murmur at that, and yet be loyal. It distresses us to know that the murmurs of these men pierced the heart of Christ; that the iron entered into His soul when they would not receive the word of life which He gave them; then may our loyalty be pleasant to our King, and may no murmuring of ours wound Him. 'doth this cause you to stumble?'

(v. 62) 'What then if ye should behold the Son of Man ascending where he was before?' 'Would ye then be convinced,' our

Lord seems to say, 'that the things I have said to you are real things and not dreams; that mine is indeed a glory greater than that of any earthly king; or would ye still harden your hearts and say that your concern is not with the Son of man, or with heaven, but is only for 'what ye shall eat and what ye shall drink and wherewithal ye shall be clothed'?

(v. 63) 'It is the spirit that quickeneth.' Here is the interpretation of the hard saying. 'The words that I have spoken unto you are spirit and are life.'[233] We might suppose that all difficulties would vanish once it was understood that no impossible corporeal eating or drinking was intended; but in truth the saying becomes harder for us all when we face it in its full significance. That 'the flesh profiteth nothing,' is no matter, is the lesson which individuals and nations are set to learn by means of famine and sword, sickness and disaster. Now and then we get a glimmering of the truth when the tale of some heroic act reaches us, or when, in our worst distress, the comfort of God finds us. But, for the most part the everyday business of our lives is carried on with the notion that we live in order to provide, for ourselves, and for 'our flesh and blood,' all things for the needs, or the luxuries, or the glorification of the flesh. Only a saint of God here and there, like S. Francis of Assissi, is able to realise the full measure of this saying; and probably just so far as we can understand that 'the flesh profiteth nothing,' whether in the way of pampering it or of mortifying it, shall we be able to comprehend what this other saying means, 'it is the spirit that quickeneth.' Then shall we sustain our souls in gladness upon every word of Christ: we shall eat and live, because His words 'are spirit, and are life.'[234]

---

[233] Here is the interpretation for the hard saying, the key that explains the whole, the words are spirit and are life; eating means receiving the Word.

[234] Mason, by implication, rejects transubstantiation or any other view which would imply literal corporeal eating.

(v. 64) Here we get a glimpse into the inner mind of our Lord. All the time as he walked up and down with the band of disciples, who had chosen Him as much as He had chosen them, He carried the consciousness that some would not believe, and that one should betray, and yet all the time He strove against their unbelief with human hopefulness. But now He challenges the faithless and disloyal—'but there are some of you that believe not;'[235] He unmasked them to themselves; they were no longer to halt between two opinions; the hour of their probation had gone by.

(v. 65) They could not respond to the final test; they were not drawn to Christ by the Father, but in seeking Him they were self-seekers. It is well for us to remember that our Lord would have from us a generous surrender as well as a loyal devotion; that he will not always be patient with our half-avowed intention to take religion seriously some day when other things are less pressing. May no sordid meanness on our part in the things of our religion add to the disappointments of Christ.

(v. 66) Our Lord's words take effect on this occasion as when he said—'That thou doest, do quickly.' He came 'that the thoughts of many hearts should be revealed.[236] 'Upon this, many of His disciples went back.' They had lost all hope of preferment from One who had come to be in their eyes a mere mystic, a dreamer, incapable of even discerning the things which were of real consequence. They go back to pick up their former affairs and to make the best of this world in their own way. 'And walked no more with Him.' The phrase is tender and pathetic, suggesting how 'Over whose acres walked those blessed feet'[237] in noonday heat and in the weariness of eventide, always with the following of disciples. 'Walked with'—the phrase used in village life when a man and a woman choose each other and take time to know each

[235] They were rejecting the bread he offered.

* Luke 1:36.

[237] Shakespeare, *King Henry the IV*, Part 1: Act 1, Scene 1.

other before the final choice for better, for worse. What a tender intimate suggestion of the disciples' relations with our Lord! How rude and sore the desertion—a foretaste of the hour when all His disciples forsook him and fled. 'behold and see if there be any sorrow like unto My sorrow!'²³⁸* (v. 67) 'Would ye also go away? He asks of the Twelve. Could words be more pathetic, more full of the shame and dejection of desertion?

(v. 68) 'Lord, to whom shall we go?' that Simon Peter should twice have had the honour of announcing the faith of Christendom!²³⁹ His faith cheers us; we are so very glad he said the words we would fain have said had we been there. 'whom have I in Heaven but Thee? And there is none upon earth that I desire in comparison of Thee.'²⁴⁰ He understands with a great faith that there is but one precious thing in the world, one thing of ultimate value, and that that thing is *words*;²⁴¹ those words of eternal life which Christ has, which Christ had just let fall to the full feeding and satisfying of noble heart at any rate. 'We believe and are sure that Thou art the Holy One of God.' Happy for the Twelve that they had a spokesman who saw in one flash of faith this great truth by which men live, and happy for the Apostle that he had words wherewith to comfort the sadness of Christ! We expect a cordial answer which should show that the burden was lifted some what from the spirit of our Master; but there are in all our lives moments of dejection so deep that comfort fails to find us; Christ answered, 'did not I choose you the Twelve, and one of you is a devil? He spake of Judas.' It is a little the fashion in our day to

---

** Lamentations 1:12.

²³⁹ The Christian faith is here summed up: 'thou hast the words of eternal life'. v. 68 has the equivalent declaration of Peter 'thou art the Christ, the Son of the living God.'

²⁴⁰ Whom have I in heaven but thee? and there is none upon earth that I desire beside thee. Psalms 73:25.

²⁴¹ Words are things of ultimate value; and above all the Word of Christ.

find extenuating circumstances until black shades off into grey, if not into spotless white; Christ speaks the terrible fact—'One of you,' not, will become, but, 'is a devil' Knowing this, our Lord suffered the man to go in and out with Him to the end; was it to give him every conceivable chance of recovery? We wonder what the effect of this saying was upon the Twelve: later on, when their training was more nearly finished, when they had learnt self-distrust and humility, each one asked, Lord, is it I? Now, perhaps, they eyed each other askance, wondering who was the 'devil' in their midst.

SCALE HOW 'MEDITATIONS'

Dominus Illuminatio Mea

No. 26
(S. John 7:1-13)

THE FEAST OF TABERNACLES[242]

(v. 1) 'After these things.' The Evangelist covers a space of six months in this phrase in which many miracles had been performed, as the healing of the Syro-Phoenician woman's daughter, of the deaf and dumb man, the feeding of the four thousand, the restoring of the blind man at Bethsaida. Peter had made his second great confession. The three had witnessed the transfiguration; and much teaching of the things of the kingdom had been given. The result of Christ's work was that his position had become more and more unsafe. 'Jesus walked in Galilee, for He would not walk in Judea, because the Jews (*i.e.* religious leaders of the people) sought to kill Him.'

(v. 2) 'Now the feast of the Jews, 'etc., the feast of Tabernacles, the most popular of all the feasts, the autumn thanksgiving held in remembrance of the time when the people dwelt in tents, was at hand.

---

[242] Mason, "The Feast of Tabernacles" *The Parents' Review* 20, no. 4 (April 1909): 305-308.

(v. 3) 'His brethren,' variously surmised to be His cousins, the sons of the Virgin's sister, or the children of Joseph by a former marriage.[243] They have followed His teaching, step by step; surely, one would say, they ought to know; and they are not convinced. It is worth while in our own family and social relations to remember this fact, lest we, too, think slight things of the worthiest amongst us. The Greatest could live amongst men and not be recognised even by His own family; they looked for signs of mastery, and He gave them signs of meekness; they looked for a ruler, and He said, 'I am among you as He that serveth,' and they did not know Him, and were puzzled and baffled by the signs which they saw. Still, the family credit was much to them, and they take it upon them to chide him. 'Why walk in Galilee any longer? Depart hence, and go into Judea; where are the priests and the scribes able to discern by sure signs whether a man be a prophet or no.' Also it would seem that the following of Christ had decreased, and that in Judea they might again be recovered, for the brethren add, 'that thy disciples also may behold thy works.'

(v. 4) 'For no man doeth anything in secret.' We see how little they had apprehended our Lord's teaching as to that which is done by the right hand not being known by the left hand. They see no object in the teaching and work of Christ except as a proclamation of Himself and His personal claims. They are yet in the outer darkness of those who believe that 'to get on' is the chief thing in life; to get on by fair means, if they can, but by all means to get on. Their charge against Christ appears to be that He had in no way bettered the position of Himself or his family by all the signs and wonders He had done. There is nothing more limiting to the horizon, more blinding to the inward eye, than this habit of placing personal or family advancement before us as a final aim. We feel that it is virtuous and praiseworthy to do the best we can

---

[243] Mason affirms the interpretation consistent with the perpetual Virginity of Mary.

for ourselves and for our own, and our eyes are blinded 'that we see not the truth.' 'If thou doest these things.'—From chiding they pass easily into scoffing and doubting. The very works they had seen with their own eyes were no longer certain to them until they had received the stamp of the world's acceptance. This is one of the dangers of pursuing the favours of the world; and here, perhaps, we have the secret of much of the light scepticism of the present day. It is not that the anguish of doubt has pierced men to the soul, but that they choose to stand well with their world by thinking in advance of the most advanced and, perhaps, flippant of their set.[244] It is not the part of a loyal disciple to challenge Christ to 'manifest thyself to the world,' to ask petulantly for a solution of the baffling problems of life, but to wait his Lord's pleasure with steadfast faith.[245]

(v. 5) 'Even His brethren did not believe on Him.' The Evangelist would appear to record the fact with sadness.

(v. 6-10) Christ answers with the same sad irony which appears in 'Sleep on now, and take your rest.' Every word has grated upon Him, and every word has wounded; every word spoken by His brethren has been foreign to His nature and His aims. 'My time (for convincing the world) is not yet come.' The ages are still waiting for the full coming of that time, 'but your time (for flattering the world, waiting the world's pleasure, living for the world's approbation) is always ready.' So of us: if we live only to get on in the world, there need be no pause for recollection—we must energise continually. If we live for the service of God, we shall often have to wait long to see what God will do with us. Our time will not be alway ready. 'the world cannot hate you (because ye are its own, and no man hateth his own), but Me it Hateth, because I testify of it that its works are evil.' The very life of Christ,

---

[244] Another point of contact with the content of the draft letter: the following the crowd in their light skepticism. See below note 234.

[245] Waiting in faith is the solution to the skepticism of the age.

His goings to and fro among the people, His attitude towards men and towards God,—all this had the irritating effect of a continual protest. 'Go ye up unto the feast; I go not up yet, because my time is no yet fulfilled'; and Jesus abode in Galilee, and His brethren went up to Jerusalem, no doubt joining the festal companies of their people.

(v. 10) 'But when His brethren were gone up, then went He also up, but as it were in secret.' Perhaps of all the undesigned coincidences by which the faithfulness of S. John's record is established none is more striking than this—that he makes no attempt to explain an apparent contradiction; no attempt to reconcile what appear to be contradictory statements. Let us also not trouble ourselves with the effort to reconcile apparent discrepancies. Christ said, 'I go not up,' and yet He went up. So be it. It would be pleasant to believe that our Lord reconsidered the matter, as men do, but we are content to leave it, knowing that 'He doeth all things well.'[246]

(v. 11) 'where is He?' We are introduced to a scene of great animation, of much coming and going, of many meetings and greetings. It would be difficult to form an idea of the gay stir produced in Jerusalem at the seasons of the great feasts; especially is this true of the Feast of Tabernacles, when every man carried branches of fruits, chiefly citron. But on this occasion there is an undercurrent of intense excitement; all thoughts are turned to Christ; everyone asks of his neighbour, 'where is He?' The Jews, the Leaders of the people, sought Him to take away his life. The multitude was divided in opinion; his warmest friends appear to have no very strong convictions; they seek to defend Him from charges which would prove Him to be worse than other men; that is all. 'He is a good man,' they say. Naturally so timorous a defence carries no weight. They who are on Christ's side must ever be aggressive, and not merely on the defensive;

---

[246] There is no need to find a solution for each Scripture difficulty.

they must be inflamed with the ardour of those who follow a great leader. But these half-hearted defenders have their following to-day. 'He is a good man,' is the feeble creed of multitudes who have never been touched with the divine passion of Christianity. Nor do these see that they are making for Christ a claim which is insupportable. If he were no more than 'a good man,' then may we reverently dare to say that He was not a good man. How dare any son of man but this lift up his face and say boldly, 'I and my Father are one,' thus making himself equal with God? There is no half-way house on the Way of Life. We must venture boldly—worship Him as our God, serve Him as our King, embrace Him as our Saviour—or Christ is nothing to us.[247] 'Not so,' say the other, 'but He leadeth the multitude astray.' The charge is ever the same, that the religion of the Gospel gives the common people 'false ideas,' above all, the mischievous notion that they are of value in the eyes of God who are of no account in the eyes of men.

(v. 13) 'Howbeit no man spake openly for fear of the Jews.' All this eager discussion goes on in corners and in subdued tones. The people know the mind of their rulers very well; for fear of the Jews, the leaders of religion, they dare not speak of Him who is the Way of all true religion. Not that this fear exonerates them: who knows but, if all the disciples of Christ then gathered in Jerusalem had had the courage of their convictions and had spoken out boldly all that was in their hearts, that the rulers themselves might not have listened. We are not, perhaps, called upon to proclaim our faith upon the housetops, but this, at least, is required of us—that when the occasion arises for us to speak, our words shall carry some of the passion of our convictions.

---

[247] This serves to dispel any doubt about the kind of Christian commitment foundational to Mason and her following.

SCALE HOW 'MEDITATIONS'
Dominus Illuminatio Mea

No. 27
(S. John 7:14-24)

THE GREAT CONTROVERSY[248]

(v. 14) Christ went to the Feast as an outlaw, waiting until the roads were free of passengers, for all had gone to Jerusalem. The Jews sought His life, and He would run no unnecessary risk; while He would avoid no duty, whatever danger might attend it. In the midst of the Feast, that is on the fourth day, Christ appeared; not in the by-ways of the city, but in the heart of danger, which was also the post of duty—'He taught in the Temple.' What follows has been called the great controversy.[249] Christ stands to answer attacks from various quarters, and each attack shows a separate drift of opinion, and throws light upon the characters of the speakers.

(v. 15) 'The Jews, therefore, marvelled.' 'the Jews,' *i.e.*, the priests, the scribes, the Pharisees, the leisured class, in fact, who gave themselves to so complete an observance of the law as was not possible for men who had to earn their living. They had all received an equivalent to a university education; they had their great schools and their famous masters and their definite courses of study, the elementary stage of which occupied a youth until his

---

[248] "The Great Controversy" *The Parents' Review* 20, no. 5 (May 1909): 384-387.

* Cf. Westcott on S. John's Gospel.

twenty-first year. They spoke with the scorn of graduates for non-graduate ministers of religion: 'How knoweth this man letter, having never learned?' But they 'marvelled,' for that Jesus did know was plain even to their unwilling minds.

(v. 16) Jesus answered that He did belong to a great school with the Greatest of all teachers. He was no illiterate, no empiric; He taught with authority. 'My teaching is not mine, but his that sent me.' Then follows one of those luminous teachings of Christ which light up the whole interior life of the individual, and which show a clear solution of the problems which are for ever baffling one or another school of thought. That Christianity is not demonstrable, and is therefore not to be received, has, from the beginning until now, been the contention of scientist, philosophers, historians. Christ accepts the postulate; Christianity is not demonstrable, but is discernable only by that inward light which every man is capable of casting upon its truths. What is that light? The honest and simple will, which our Lord has already had occasion to commend. 'if any man *willeth* to do His will, he shall know of the teaching whether it be of God' (*R.V.*) conviction in this supreme matter is of the will first, and then of the intellect. He that willeth shall *know;* nor is it well we should think that willing to do the will of God is the same thing as willing what we call a career of usefulness, even of self-sacrifice. 'this is the work of God, that ye believe on Him whom He hath sent.'[250] Willing the will, like working the work, is, probably, to hold ourselves in that willing and obedient attitude of soul in which conviction is possible; to keep the single eye, to ponder upon the things of Christ, without giving place to pride of intellect, whether it be in refuting or in confirming the truth by which we live. To this attitude of soul comes faith—the free gift of God. He shall *know* of the doctrine, *know* with absolute assurance. Nor is this as some would say, a kind of mental conjuring, impossible to

---

* S. John 6.29.

the honest mind which would prefer to face every doubt and every difficulty. It is thus that all our great convictions come to us. By this receptivity—the highest function of the spiritual intelligence[251] —we know whatever we do know of the deeper meanings of life and love and eternity. It is not by his actions or the proofs we get of his affection, that we really know a human friend. We know him when we regard him with the single eye and will to see him as he truly is, that is, at his best; for the law of our being is one law, whether we would discern one another or discern the Christ of God. The time comes when proofs and evidences are to be left aside as having served their purpose, and we see with that inward light which our Lord describes as the single will. 'If any man *willeth* to do His will He shall *know*,' and we all know that this is true. A flash of conviction, an impulse of the higher life, will cause a man to throw over the most promising prospects and go, he knows not whither, to do, he knows not what; as Abram and Matthew, the publican, when each received his call. This, if we will believe it, is the very *crux* of Christianity; That it is not to be proven; and is yet self-proven, inevitable, to him who will receive it.

(v. 18) 'He that speaketh from himself seeketh his own glory.' Our Lord continues His refutation of that charge of the Jews, that he was a self-elected teacher, a man who had never learned. At the same time He carries on His teaching regarding the doctrine of the potent will. What was the aim of the teaching of Christ? did He come to magnify himself? Was self-exaltation, material, intellectual, spiritual, His object, or was He not rather the sole son of man who has ever been able to say,—'I am meek an lowly of heart?' it is only as an ambassador, honoured for his sovereign's sake, that Christ claims confidence. 'He that seeketh the glory of Him that sent Him the same is true.' Here, perhaps, is the secret

---

[251] The highest function of the spiritual intelligence is willingness to receive God's word through meditation.

of the will, impotent to believe, and to know the truth of the
doctrine. The intellectual arrogance, 'the strife for triumph more
than truth,' the sense that nothing can be, shall be, true, which is
not open to proof by recognised intellectual methods, this
unconscious self-glorification is as a veil between even the honest
and good heart and the truth which is to be discerned by quite
other methods. Worse is his case who does not *will* to do the will
of the Father because he has private ends of his own to
accomplish, things to get and to have, a position to make, his own
glory to seek. He cannot withdraw himself from himself and look
at that which is invisible; he cannot know of the doctrine whether
it be of God.[252]

(v. 19) We come to another point in the great controversy with
the Jews. 'Did not Moses give you the law and yet none of you
doeth the law? Why seek ye to kill Me? The law had become the
sole religion of the Jews, had obscured for them the gracious
vision of the Law-giver who gives laws to men as a father gives
rules to his children to save them from hurtful wrong-doing.
Losing the conception of the Law-giver, they lose all sense of
proportion in their regard for the law and would break the sixth
commandment of the moral law to punish the breach of a mere
traditional gloss on the fourth.

(v. 21-24) The Jews make no answer. The question of Christ,
'Why seek ye to kill Me?' revealed the purpose they had supposed
hidden; but the 'multitude' of pilgrims, come up for the feast,
carry on the controversy. They know nothing of the intention of
the rulers, and ask 'Who seeketh to kill Thee?' and taunt Christ
with demoniacal possession because he has this notion—'Thou
hast a devil.' Christ, in answer, pursues the controversy, which
turned on the miracle of the impotent man whom He made every

---

[252] Mason expresses her criticism of utilitarian rationalism and theological
liberalism and explains why intellectual arrogance darkens the will in such a way
that asking for proof becomes an obstacle for the knowledge of truth.

whit whole on the Sabbath day. 'If circum cision, an act of wounding, is lawful on the Sabbath, are ye wrath with me because I made a man every whit whole on the Sabbath?' We seem to notice a greater tenderness and gentleness in our Lord's words when He speaks to the multitude. They are not blinded by prejudice; they are not seeking to kill Him; they are open to conviction, and He labours with divine gentleness to make them see the truth.

(v. 24) 'Judge not according to appearances, but judge righteous judgment.' Here again our Lord appeals to that inner power of discerning truth, which all men possess, and for which all men are responsible. Appearances, proofs, evidences—how misleading they are in all things human and divine! Used in strict subordination to that power of judging, that will to do and to see, that inner witness which every man possesses, they serve their purpose; but, apart from this judging of righteous judgement, how futile they are! Our laws hold fast divine truth so far anyway that they do not convict a man upon circumstantial evidence.

No. 28

THE GREAT CONTROVERSY (Part II)
(S. John 7:25-35)[253]

(v. 25-27) 'Some of them of Jerusalem.' The original would perhaps correspond to such a phrase as 'some Londoners.' These were better informed than the multitude of pilgrims; they are aware that there is a conspiracy amongst the priests and rulers to take the life of Christ. Apparently he is in their hands, teaching openly in the Temple, and they not only do nothing, but 'they say nothing unto Him.' For a moment the faith of the people in their rulers is shaken. Could it be possible that their teachers, whom they held as altogether righteous, should know that here indeed was the Messiah, and should yet seek to take away His life? But that were too infamous a thing to imagine. Was not the whole Jewish people waiting for the Coming One? How then imagine that their teachers and leaders, those who knew best amongst them, were conspiring to defraud the nation of Him who should be their Peace, and to set aside the promise of God? No, this could not be; some other explanation must be sought. It was their own ignorance of Scripture that was in fault; the rulers knew well enough that this was not the Christ; for example, 'Howbeit we know this man whence He is, but when the Christ cometh no man knoweth whence He is.' The loyalty of the people to their leaders made them search for justification for their attitude towards Christ, and they appear to have had in view some such words as—'the Lord shall

---

[253] Mason, "The Great Controversy II" *The Parents' Review* 20, no. 5 (May 1909): 387-390.

suddenly come to His temple': but this was no sudden coming of an unknown great One, for did they not know His father and mother, and about His home in Nazareth? So men talked in a corner; not aloud for fear of the Jews.

(v. 28-29) But Christ, with that unerring discernment which enables him always to answer, not mere words, but the secret thoughts of His interlocutor, perceived what was being said in this perhaps distant group of men, and 'cried' to them, perhaps because they were far off, 'teaching and saying;' accepting their notion of truth for as much as it was worth; not meeting their doubts with a literal exposition of the prophecies; not testifying that they did know whence the Christ should come, that the city of David was to be also the city of the Messias, and that He, according to prophecy was indeed born in Bethlehem. This would be evidence according to the letter, and 'the letter killeth.' Our Lord adopts another line of argument raising His hearers, as always, to a higher lever of thought. 'Ye both know me and know whence I am,' he says, admitting their acquaintance with Him as one man know another; but there is more to know than ye think of. I came not of myself, but 'He that sent me is true, whom ye know not.' My life is not limited by the relations and circumstances that ye think ye know. I am sent to discover to you, in the only way in which you could comprehend it, Him who cannot err as you are erring now in your judgment of me, because He is true. 'Who ye know not'—for had ye know Him, the truth would have opened your eyes, and you would have discerned me also. 'I know Him.' 'I am from Him.' 'He sent Me.'

(v. 30) 'They sought, therefore, to take Him. 'They' probably being the rulers and their following, who watched with increasing jealousy the impression that Christ was making upon the people. 'An no man laid his hand on Him, because His hour was not yet come.' It is said that every man bears a charmed life till his work is done; how much more He, whose work is the salvation of the world.

(v. 31) 'but of the multitude many believed on Him.' 'the multitude,' the country people come up for the feast appear to be the most accessible of the several parties. They appear to have the candour, the openness of mind, which is the first condition of conviction. They recount the miracles that Christ had done to their knowledge; this one telling one tale of wonder, another (from Nain It may be) a more marvellous story, until the tide of conviction spread amongst them, and they said, —'When the Christ shall come, will He do more signs than those which this man hath done?' Theirs was an elementary faith founded upon signs and wonders; there is no hint that they had the spiritual insight which penetrated beneath the signs to the gracious mystery which underlay them all—the presence among men of the divine son of God.

(v. 32) Still their conviction seems to have been sincere so far as it went and the ever watchful Pharisees heard, with increasing hatred of their Victim, this talk amongst the people. They are not to be restrained any more by considerations of prudence, by a fear of a general rising in favour of Jesus, and by dread of the consequent interposition of the Roman power; 'the chief priests and the Pharisees sent officers to take Him;' the 'officers' probably whose business it was 'to take' or to expel disorderly offenders from the precincts of the Temple.

(v. 33) Christ arraigns them in turn, thought they probably do not see the force of His arraignment. 'Jesus therefore,' *i.e.,* because they had committed the offence against His august Person of sending against Him the officers whose concern was with the common breakers of the law, as though, to compare a lesser thing with an infinitely greater, a posse of policemen were sent to apprehend the Prince of Wales; Jesus therefore said,—yet a little while I am with you, and I go unto Him that sent me.' Did ever ambassador withdraw from an unfriendly country with such sovereign dignity? But the withdrawal is complete; these words appear to mark the point when Christ ceases for the time to strive with the Jews as a nation. He foretells His speedy withdrawal to the courts of heaven whence He came.

(v. 34) 'Ye shall seek me and shall not find me.' The time should come, as we know it did in the siege of Jerusalem, when the rulers should bethink themselves of Christ, and should go out after many false Messiahs in the belief that each was this Jesus whom they crucified. 'and where I am ye cannot come.' No, because were Christ is, is ever a condition and not a place. No change of place should remove Him from instant access to the meek and lowly of heart who come unto Him, to them who labour and are heavy-laden; but to the proud and the prejudiced, the wilful and undisciplined, to all after the kind of these Pharisees and priests, the word is still true—'Where I am ye cannot come.'

(v. 35) Again, 'the letter killeth.' The Jews could find none but a literal meaning in the words of Christ. 'Whither will this Man go that we shall not find Him?' 'Will He go unto the Dispersion among the Greeks?' that is, to the Jews scattered through Syria and southern Europe; those Jews to whom S. Paul first addressed himself when he entered into the cities where they were scattered. 'And teach the Greeks.' We seem to hear the bitterness of scorn with which these words are pronounced; will this outcast from among His own people carry His strange doctrine to the Gentiles? That were a fitting end for such as He. How human and living is the picture of passionate irritation we get in—'What is the word that He said? Ye shall seek me and shall not find me, and where I am ye cannot come.' But we perceive that the words have lodged; they repeat them with finger pointed, lips writhed in derision, but never more will they be able to forget. 'Where I am ye cannot come,' will echo and re-echo henceforth in those hearts as the death-knell of the better possibilities of their lives. The controversy with the Jews, the leaders, that is, is practically closed; the final words have been spoken. If it should happen to any one of us to be in controversy with Christ at the present moment, exalting our wisdom above His wisdom, preferring our way to His way, our ends to His purposes, let us pause and consider betimes. He will not always strive with the children of men; it is possible for the final word to be spoken.

SCALE HOW 'MEDITATIONS'
Dominus Illuminatio Mea

No. 29

THE GREAT CONTROVERSY
(Part III)
(S. John 7:37-39)[254]

(v. 37) 'Now on the last day, the great day of the Feast.' It would appear that, while the special note of the Gospel of S. Matthew is the fulfilment of prophecy, S. John's more mystic mind was especially impressed with those discourses of our Lord in which He revealed Himself as fulfilling that which was prefigured by pictures or types, especially those types which occur during the wilderness journey of the Israelites. In S. John 6 is the discourse in which our Lord gives full interpretation to the type of manna; the water from the smitten rock, the pillar of fire by night, and the brazen serpent lifted up, all are confronted with their Antitype.

It is a question whether the last day of the Feast was the seventh day or whether it was the day of holy convocation at the end of the Feast, when the Israelites took down their tents, and when the sacrifices were more numerous, and the rejoicings even greater than throughout the Feast.

'Jesus stood and cried.' The eastern teacher sat while his disciples stood; these words give the idea of a spontaneous, irrepressible appeal, urgent, impassioned; the days of Christ's ministry were drawing to a close, and they 'would not come unto Him that they might be saved.' We must read the words that follow in connection with a custom peculiar to the Feast of Tabernacles.

---

[254] Mason, "The Great Controversy III" *The Parents' Review* 20, no. 6 (June 1909): 464-467.

When the morning sacrifices were laid upon the altar, a priest went to the Pool of Siloam with a golden ewer, which he filled, and returned by the Water Gate. As he approached the altar, he did so through ordered ranks of the people in their best attire, each holding the *lûlâb* (*i.e.* bunch of green boughs) in one hand and the citron fruit on the other. As he ascended the steps the trumpets blew a triumphant blast, and the people shouted; then the water was poured into a silver basin. At night the people met again to rejoice over this ceremony of water bearing, men and women, in the Women's Court; and a Jewish proverb runs, 'He who has never seen the rejoicing at the pouring out of the water of Siloam has never seen rejoicing in his life.' We who read wonder how much this image meant to the Jews. They know how Moses struck the rock twice, and living water gushed out, and the stream followed the people trough their wilderness journey. They knew how the prophets had again and again made reference to this living water,—'Ho, every one that thirsteth, come ye to the waters.'[255] No doubt they understood in a dim way that this living water imaged the Messias who should come; though perhaps they did not understand in the fullness of S. Paul's later teaching,—'They drank of the spiritual Rock which followed them, and that Rock was Christ.'[256]

'If any man thirst, let him come unto Me, and drink.' And now the crowded congregation in the Temple hear amazing words, words fitly described by those 'officers' when they say, 'never man so spake.' If any man, anywhere, through all the world, at any time, throughout the ages, if *any* man thirst, if any man is faint and wary, exhausted, or feverish, in his journey through this troublesome world, let him come unto Me, saith Christ, and drink. We in western climes have, for the most part never thirsted, and have no conception of the utter satisfaction, the complete

---

* Isaiah 55:1.

* 1 Cor. 10:4.

rehabilitation that comes of drinking. It is in their thirst men realise that there is but one thing to drink in the world, whether we get our water from udder of the cow, or from the juice of the grape, however we flavour it and adulterate it, or whether we drink it pure and fresh from the spring. There is but one satisfaction for this most intense of our physical needs, as there is but one draught for that parching thirst of the spirit of which Christ, who know all things, testifies. 'I drank, drank, drank,' says one who was athirst, 'one can of water after another; I felt how the thick blood again flowed easily through my veins; how my hands, which were before shrivelled up like pieces of wood, swelled; how my skin became moist and perspired, how my whole body received new life and new strength.' Such is the joy of drinking, drinking, when one is a prey to thirst. There is a worse thirst than this of the body;—when all vital forces seem to have collapsed; when one would fain, like the child Ishmael, lie down and die; when nothing seems worth while; when to do the same thing, to see the same objects, day after day, palls on our very soul; when the people we know are a wariness; when life is arid; when discontent and despondency, or drearier indifference, or burning anxiety, or the fever of excitement or dissipation, fall upon us,—then, we thirst. We do not know what ails us. Change of friends or change of scene, money or leisure, hold for us, so we think, the satisfaction we need. But if our spirit be finely touched, we find in these only passing alleviations; the thirst comes on us again; for it is indeed that divine discontent to which the psalmist gives voice,—'My soul is athirst for God, for the living God.' It is because He knows of this thirst of all men every where, and because He knows that in Himself is the divine fullness of life which is the only satisfaction for the thirsting souls of men, that Christ, thirsting also for men as they thirst for Him. With great love and desire, cries aloud—'If any man thirst, let him come unto Me, and drink.' It is only in the drinking, the personal appropriation, that full satisfaction comes, and 'our peace flows as a river.' Never before and never since in the history of the world has such a proffer been made to mankind.

Only He who is named by the highest Name could, without the extremity of blasphemous folly, make such an offer to a fainting world. Is it mystical, no to be understood by plain people who rely upon their common sense? On the contrary, here again, the law of our life is one law. The satisfaction Christ offers is, in kind, like that refreshment for spirit which we can occasionally give to one another; but in degree it differs; for it is infinite, complete, eternal; and not for one or two, or half-a dozen, but for all. We weary ourselves with the shows of things and shrink from the very bliss of a plunge into the real.

(v. 38) 'He that believeth on Me.' 'Believing' is used as synonymous with drinking,—unreserved acceptance. 'As the Scripture hath said.' The reference appears to be to the rock in the wilderness, and to all subsequent teaching founded upon that story. 'Out of his belly shall flow rivers of living water.' He who drinks shall himself be as a spring in the desert, following freely and unconsciously, and in its turn satisfying the thirst of all comers. The figure appears to point to the natural Christian life, and not to any effort of preaching or teaching.[257] Perhaps a certain hopefulness and gladness and freshness of living, a sparkle as of spring water, is especially characteristic of Christian people.

(v. 39) 'But this spake He of the Spirit.' The Evangelist appears to think that this saying asks for interpretation. This outflow of life was to take place after the day of Pentecost, when the Spirit of Christ should descend upon the disciples of Christ. We begin to understand when, for the outflow of living water, we substitute the more familiar 'fruits of the Spirit'—; love, joy, peace, long-suffering, gentleness, meekness, goodness, temperance. 'Jesus was not yet glorified.' The immediate glorification was that of the cross—'I, If I be lifted up.'

---

[257] Christian life flows without effort, and blesses others.

SCALE HOW 'MEDITATIONS'

Dominus Illuminatio Mea

No. 30
(S. John 7:40-50)[258]

(v. 40) 'Some of the multitude.' Now for the first time we find the 'multitude'—the pilgrims assembled for the Feast—divided. Some said, —'this is of a truth the prophet,' that is, the prophet foretold by Moses, 'a prophet shall the Lord your God raise up unto you, like unto me; unto him shall ye hearken.'—We admire the temerity of their avowal, an avowal made at great risk to themselves. At the same time, these choose the least aggressive way of confessing the faith that is in them. 'Other,' gaining greater courage from the boldness of the first speakers, venture all in a word, an said (we may conceive with what solemnity of voice and manner),—'this is the Christ.' this bold avowal strikes the note of division among the multitude, and we find them divided, as men have been ever since, into those who recognise truth by its own light and those who require truth to be illuminated by light from without; those who receive the inner witness, and those who will be convinced only by external evidence, whether historic or scientific. That seventeenth century saint, *Brother Lawrence,* is reported to have said,—That we ought to make a great difference between the acts of the *understanding* and those of the *will*; that the first were comparatively of little value, and the other all.'[259] In this

---

[258] Mason, "The Great Controversy III" *The Parents' Review* 20, no. 6 (June 1909): 467-470.

[259] That we ought to make a great difference between the acts of the understanding and those of the will; that the first were comparatively of little value, and the others all. That our only business was to love and delight ourselves in GOD. Brother Lawrence, *The Practice of the Presence of God*: Second Conversation.

multitude, as in all gatherings of men, we have those who learn to their own *understanding* and those who by an act of *will* recognise Christ.

(v. 42) In the first class we have the sceptical, whose arguments are specious, and, from their own point of view, incontrovertible; as here (v. 42),—'hath not the Scripture said that the Christ cometh of the seed of David and from Bethlehem.' The Evangelist takes no pains to point out that these people erred from an insufficient knowledge even of the facts to which they pin their faith; he is content to leave them to their intellectual difficulties; but the incident offers a lesson for us to-day. Perhaps, for example a completer knowledge of what we call the laws of nature would silence once and for all the objections of those who believe that, in the words of *Robert Elsmere*,—'miracles do not happen.'[260] But the temper of students, both of natural science and of historical criticism, is becoming daily more candid and gentle; they are less and less disposed, to believe that the last word has been spoken, are more open to the conviction that fuller light might resolve their doubts.[261]

---

[260] This is an important reference, linking this thought with those presented ten years earlier in another unpublished manuscript, I have identified as the "draft letter". This Draft discusses in detail Mason's response to the reading of the controversial novel *Robert Elsemere* in 1888. The novel presents the story of a young clergyman who abandons the ministry of the Church of England to become an activist for social justice. This novel is an ideal reading to understand the religious context Mason had in mind in her search for educational answers by which Christian parents and teachers could respond to the crisis of faith characteristic of Late-Victorian society. The Draft Letter can be found on Mason's Achieve: Box CM3, The Armitt Library, Ambleside.

[261] 'Robert Elsmere, for instance, loses his head entirely on the assumption that 'miracles do not happen.' now it really should not be hard to fortify my children against such an attack as this. They must learn physical science, not only for the joy of reading the open secrets of nature, but that they may know and go safely in the knowledge, -how extremely little is open as yet to the most patient investigation; how soon we come to a blank wall in any field we follow; how we know nothing yet of fundamental truths-where and what is life? for

(v. 44) 'And some of them would have taken him.' Is it a fact that error, based upon an act of the intellect, tends to make men vindictive? If this is so in any degree, it is only because intellectual conviction is of its nature absolute; a contrary conclusion to that which he has arrived at is unthinkable to the convinced man. The law of intellectual progress seems to be conditioned something in the same way as progress down a winding lake, where again and again, your boat seems to be hemmed in by the final shore. It is possible that the courage of convictions—of certainty—is necessary to stimulate intellectual progress; the contest is for truth and not for triumph; those on the other side appear as enemies to truth, and the hatred they excite is hatred of error. We see this general principle working in the 'multitude' among whom that amazing word of our Lord's has fallen,—'If any man thirst, let him come unto Me and drink; 'It is quick and powerful to the dividing asunder of soul and spirit; as in that other case when His disciples said,—'this is a hard saying; who can hear it?' The multitude that had been with Him until now sought to take Him: they were convinced that the 'Jews' were right after all, and that this Man was an enemy to religion; but 'no man laid hands on Him.' Something, we know not what, of ineffable in the presence of

---

instance the life of a man or a plant. In protoplasm, which consists of this and that? Yes, but put this and that together in due proportions to make (life) protoplasm, and - life is not there. Not impossibly the next turn of the wheel will find us spending our strength in renewed search for that elixir- the hope of the past. Then, for the miracle of resurrection, who shall say that it is impossible whilst science knows so little of the miracle of birth; Laws of nature? how few of them we know! and who is to determine therefore, what is, or is not a miracle? This ground at any rate, the most advanced (and sceptical) of our scientist have reached: they decline to say that miracles do not happen: and affirm only that the Bible miracles have not been proved to their satisfaction: a quite different matter and by no means the last word on the subject- for those who have read much of the eclectic literature proper to the most advanced thinkers. Here are miracles of today which make the outsider (believer) smile remembering the old charge, that skepticism and superstition go hand in hand.' Mason, *Draft Letter* 13-14.

Christ kept from His person the sacrilegious hands of the enraged people.

(v. 45) 'The officers therefore came to the chief priests and Pharisees.' It would appear that the Sanhedrin was in session; possibly a special meeting had been called to deal with what the Jews felt to be a national emergency. The rulers waited with, we may believe, feverish and fretful anxiety for the return of the official whom they had sent out earlier to apprehend Jesus; at last these return, but without a prisoner. 'why did ye not bring Him?' they cry; but these men, the creatures of the Sanhedrin, the last of whom we should expect that supreme act of *will* which lays the mind open to the truth,—these men had watched and they had listened, and to them it was given to speak the final word in all controversies which would find some other place of honour for Christ than that which He claims for Himself; which would describe Him as a good man, a prophet if you will, but no more. The one answer to all such insidious opposition is contained in the words of these servants of the Temple—'Never man so spake.'

(v. 47) 'The Pharisees therefore,' etc. The rulers forget their dignity; they condescend to angry discussion with their own servants. 'Are ye also led astray? Hath any of the rulers believed on Him, or the Pharisees?' None had declared himself, any way, so rigorous were the laws towards the excommunicate. The Western Church, at its worst, never knew how to pile terrors on excommunicated persons so extreme as those employed by the rulers of the Jews, because the Western nations had long cease to retain the tribal character which the Jews have never lost. Therefore the Sanhedrin kept themselves a close body, without defection, so they thought, and poured scorn upon 'this multitude' which 'knows not the law.' The habit of regarding the 'common people' is a great test of the Christian status of a nation. When the Revolution was due in France, the 'multitude' were the *canaille*; we in England are learning, year by year, an ever greater respect for the people;[262] but the Jews, sharply divided into those who know the Law, and the ignorant, treated the latter with unmeasured scorn. They were 'accursed,' not to be touched, hardly to be spoken with.

(v. 50) 'Nicodemus saith.' We can conceive the dismay of the council when one of themselves dared to utter a protest; we are glad, because we have met with Nicodemus before and only wish that his protest had been less feeble. He attempts no defence of Jesus, but falls back on the civil law of the Jews, and proposes to defend that. 'Doth our law judge a man except it first hear from himself?' but like all half-hearted advocates he reveals his own mind without helping his cause. The Pharisees turn upon, with what bitterness we may imagine,—'Art thou also of Galilee?' Then, as now, it would seem to be the way to damn a cause by an opprobrious epithet; to fix this word of scorn, a Galilaean, upon the followers of Christ should be a sure way to injure His cause. 'Search and see that out of Galilee ariseth no prophet.' It is curious to note that all the charges against Jesus, all the arguments against His claims to be the Christ, have narrowed themselves to this, namely, that He was of Galilee, where as the Christ should come out of Judea. The Evangelist makes no comment; by their own words they are condemned. With this scene in the Sanhedrin ends the part of our Lord's momentous controversy with the Jews.

---

[262] Mason makes a quick reference to the social conflicts between the classes in Late-Victorian England.

A NEW YEAR'S MEDITATION

"Blessed are the—"

By The Editor[263]

Master, Thou will'st me poor—
Haughty and rich am I;
In self-dependence rich,
Presuming, hard, and high:
Faith, looking on the coming years, doth see
Dark faults, sore failures, let to humble me.
Thy Will be done!

A mourner must I be:
And Holy messengers
Oft have Thy presence left,
To bring me blessed tears:
Too soon they fail, and sin's hot breath sweeps by:
Then wilt Thou take the spot and show it me,
Till weeping, fain I turn to hide in Thee:
Thy Will be Done!

Meek wouldst Thou have Thy child:
How little can I bear!
How seldom wait for Thee,
Quiet, within Thy care!
Though through provokings, teach me to endure,
Bid errors make me of myself less sure.
Thy will be done!

A Hung'ring, thirsting one
Must Thy disciple be;
And I so full! Grown fat
On Thy gifts, leaving Thee!
But Thou will teach me want, or take away
All lesser bread, till Thou, my only stay:
Thy will be done!

---

[263] Mason, *The Parent's Review* 16, No. 1 (January, 1905): 1-2.

Merciful as Thou art:
Oh, how hard judgments rise!
Oh, this censorious tongue,
Evil-discerning eyes!
Yet His sweet mercy will my King impart,
If by no other way, e'en through the smart
Of pity withheld in my extremities:
Thy will be done!

Pure, e'en in Thy pure eyes:
Single and free from guile;
Oh, when shall these vain thoughts
Pure rising, meet Thy smile?
E'en this, through Thee, is mine: though it should be
That, first, through purging fires, Thou go with me:
Thy will be done!

Ruled by the Prince of Peace:
How far from this my state—
Oft striving for my own,
Exacting, harsh, irate.
No peace is found in me; but Thou wilt come
And make this chafing bosom Thy sweet home:
Thy will be done!

Thus I abide his time;
For hath the king not sworn
That all these shall be mine,
And will not He perform?
If tender ways shall serve, such wilt Thou use;
But smite, if need be; I would not refuse;
Thy will be done!

SCALE HOW 'MEDITATIONS'

Dominus Illuminatio Mea

SOME NOTES OF THE EATER DAY 'MEDITATIONS' [264]
1921

By C. M. Mason

What a grand opening to the Collect for Easter Day!- 'opened the gate of everlasting life.' We rather expect after going through all the hopes of Easter to pass on to something large and great and wonderful, and we find a prayer that any one can use at any time- 'Put into our minds good desires.'[265] Easter takes away all anxiety, all uneasiness, all self-reproach; we are all taken into the supreme joy of Easter-time. What desires do we ask for? 'If ye then be risen with Christ seek those things that are above.'[266] Things without shape or substance –the things that influence life– the fruits of the spirit.

---

[264] Mason, "Some Notes of the Eater Day, Meditations" *The Parents' Review* 36, no. 4 (April 1925): 234-237.

[265] The Collect for Easter: Almighty God, who through thine only-begotten Son Jesus Christ hast overcome death, and opened unto us the gate of everlasting life: We humbly bessech thee, that, as by thy special grace preventing us thou dost put into our minds good desires, so by thy continual help we may bring the same to good effect; through Jesus Christ our Lord, who liveth and reigneth with thee and the Holy Ghost, ever one God, world without end. *Amen.*

[266] Epistle Lesson for Easter according to the proper readings appointed in the Book of Common Prayer.

The note of Easter Day is joy – Resurrection. We say, 'I believe in the Resurrection of the Dead.' What do we believe? It is part of the creed for which Christians have died, and it means so much that it is difficult to put it into words. We think of the rising of the body and can only understand it by that recognition which is part of our creed. It is a mystery to be believed and adored, and the words come as a trumpet sound. St. Paul helps us: 'That which thou sowest is not quickened except it die: and that which thou sowest, thou sowest not that body that shall be, but bare grain, it may chance of wheat, or of some other grain: but God giveth it a body as it hath pleased him, and to every seed his own body.' (1 Cor. 15. 36-38) Think of an ear of corn which is not quickened unless it dies, and remember that the resurrection is more than an event: it is a principle. Again, the resurrection is not a thing of the future, it is *now*. The true message of this great Easter joy is 'There is no death' – only the flesh can die.

There is much discussion as to what happens after death.

Our Lord's word is 'To-day thou shall be with me in Paradise,' and St. John says, 'They shall follow the Lamb.' There is no death; in Christ shall all be made alive; but not in the same order, and we may be sure that all who have not feared to die will find their way to Christ. Again. 'With what body are the dead raised?' God gives us a body, still a body, still our own body, but in the sense that the corn in the ear after it has died has a resurrection body. I think we are living in wonderful times not only because God is teaching us wonderful lessons, but also because great, happy, spiritual truths are coming to the fore, and some of us believe that we may be allowed to go on with the work we have done. Perhaps it is not only the successors who carry on the work, but the spiritual thought of those who began the work. It is so good to think that any good work we carry on will be carried on. But Spirit is absolutely invisible and inaudible-no sense of ours can apprehend Spirit—it cannot be seen, touched or heard, -we only know that 'My Father worketh hitherto and I work.'

Our life is infinitely rich and, in the resurrection life, we rise to newness of life. How do we know that we shall go on increasing? There is a something which we are never going to lose. We increase in power we increase in joy. The resurrection must be so much more full. If we love on earth, enjoy beauty, glory in sweet sounds, heroic deeds, we shall glory, enjoy and love, much more in the life to come.

People wonder whether personality will be preserved. Every seed –*his own body*. Every one has some grains of sweetness that we would not part with for the world. This chapter 1 Cor. 15, is a difficult one, and there is an easier account in one of the Gospels – a story explanation, as all our Lord's stories are. Let us turn to the raising of Lazarus.[267]

In St. John 11. In verse 25, we get the most wonderful and gracious words we possess: 'I am the Resurrection and the Life.' These two things are *in* Christ, these two things *are* Christ, things we cannot show-but they are principles, and we can understand principles. As the water of life finds the dry grain, dry roots, and they spring to life and grow, so Christ is the Life. When we fail, when we are unhappy, when things go wrong, let us not fear, there is always the Resurrection. When our hearts are sick and sad, when we think no one can help: when we think no one can help in the present sorrow of Europe: when we see the image of the earthly in evil action, in evil presence, let us remember there is a resurrection coming, always coming. We may not live to see it, but the peace of God will come.

Let us see how Browning treats the subject of Resurrection in *Easter Day,* and how Tennyson writes of it in *In Memoriam.*

Miss Mason then read from 'The Saviour of the World, 'Book v. *The Raising of Lazarus.*

---

[267] A Gospel Lesson for Easter.

Lxxx

As fluttering birds jus 'scaped the nest,
Half blinded, baffled, by wide air,
Make tiny flight, then sink to rest
Fall'n in some ditch which chances there;-
E'en so our timid fancies fare
In that vast ocean of deep thought
Thou launches us upon; -scarce dare
We seize a hope we ne'er had sought,
Or hold secure the bliss that Word to men hath brought!
I am the light,' we think we see;
'I am the door,' we peer within;
I am the life.' Lord, ever be
Our life to save from death of sin!
'I am the resurrection,' win
We, for all our thinking, scarce,
A hing of all enclosed within
The casket of that word; nay, worse,
Vain words of would-be faith, like Martha, we rehearse.

Lxxxi

Pospone we till some far-off day-
The last great day when men shall rise-
Marvel, the master would display
Constant before our wondering eyes:-
The life we hold in him defies
Death's last assault; we go to bed;
In dust awhile our body lies;
Our friends bewail us; whilst we're led
By our Risen Lord to seats whence Death flies,
vanquishéd.
And every day, behold, we fall;

But, lo, that germ of life we hold
May not be weighted by the pall
Of custom or of death as cold;
We rise, in our Redeemer bold;
Where there is life needs it must rise;
No cerement shall the soul enfold;
The strong truth lifts us to the skies;
Lo, resurrection is- our life in amplest guise.

APPENDIX I

'MEDITATION' IN "THE STORY OF CHARLOTTE MASON"

Sunday was never an out-of-doors day. It had a flavour of its own in Miss Mason's household. There was a complete rest from ordinary duties. It was not to be a day for letter writing, nor a day for making up for lost time. No strenuous expeditions were allowed, or social events. Its restfulness depended upon seemingly trivial arrangements within the house itself. The students used different rooms and had access to books of poetry, essays, biography and works of art and travel. Fine Sunday afternoons were spent in the college garden and along the Terrace Walk. The day was well filled. Church-going was compulsory and for an hour in the afternoon Miss Mason held her 'Meditations' or 'Meds.'

I found that time passed at a different pace on Sundays; there was the bliss of peaceful leisure. At Meds each student found help according to her capacity. Perhaps to some help came later when studying the life of Christ with children, using *The Saviour of the World* (Charlotte Mason's verse commentary on the Gospels). Others were shown a way in which to read the gospels dwelling upon our Lord's words and works, finding in them fresh thoughts and new hopes with which to face the needs of the coming week. Often some aspect of truth made clear at the Sunday class became the support necessary for a new and difficult experience. The centurion, who prayed to our Lord to heal his servant, was seen to be a man *under* authority. To a student about to spend a week in school, facing a group of children difficult to control, this was a strengthening idea, received with gratitude. The knowledge that authority is a real fact, having a divine source, could be remembered in a tight place.[268]

...

[268] Essex Cholmondeley, *The Story of Charlotte Mason* (London: J.M. Dent & Sons Ltd., 1960) 155-156. Cholmondeley's personal recollection of her experience as a student in the *House of Education* during 1918-1919.

In *Home and School Education* there is a paragraph upon the habit of meditation:

> Meditation is also a habit to be acquired, or rather preserved, for we believe that children are born to meditate, as they are to reflect; indeed, the two are closely allied. In reflecting we ruminate on what we have received. In meditating we are not content to go over the past, we allow our minds to follow out our subject to all its issues. It has long been known that progress in the Christian life depends much upon meditation; intellectual progress, too, depends, not on mere reading or the laborious getting up of a subject which we call study, but on that active surrender of all the powers of the mind to the occupation of the subject in hand,[269]

It would be interesting to know when Charlotte Mason first began the lifelong practice of meditation, giving to the gospel story 'that full gaze of the mind we call attention'[270] In an early letter (1861) she speaks of the difficulty of finding the best time for prayer:

Often in our prayers, at the fat-end of the day and tired out, we numble a set of words... So to remedy, so far as in me lies, two great evils, I have made up my mind as soon as tea is over, when I fell quite fresh, I will devote half or three-quarters of an hour to Bible reading and earnest prayer. I think that by thus seeking first the kingdom of heaven I shall be sure to—nay, I will say no more, lest I receive my answers in this life, and may heaven keep me from that.

Many years later Charlotte used a simple method which her students called Meditations, attentive reading of the gospel narratives, comparing them letting the mind dwell upon the

---

[269] Mason, *Home Education Series* 3:120-121.

[270] Mason, *Home Education Series* 1:156.

incidents and words, pondering their significance and then keeping the whole in mind.

...

From 1895 until 1922 Miss Mason held a Sunday class with her students, using the findings of her own meditations which she wrote day by day for many years. These Sunday 'Meditations' were printed in 1898 and were sent out to weekly subscribers. Later they were published in verse form under the title of *The Saviour of the World.* Six volumes were issued, illustrated with photographs of famous paintings many of them chosen by Miss Mason from the picture-galleries she visited abroad. She planned two last volumes but they were never finished. The 'Liberal education for all' movement in 1912 was more urgent. 'Perhaps someone will finish them when I am no longer able. My time must be given to establish what I have lived for.'[271]

---

[271] Cholmondeley, *The Story of Charlotte Mason,* 184-187.

APPENDIX II

"RABBI BEN EZRA" [272]

Rabbi Ben Ezra
Grow old along with me!
The best is yet to be,
The last of life, for which the first was made:
Our times are in His hand
Who saith 'A whole I planned,
Youth shows but half; trust God: see all, nor be afraid!'

Not that, amassing flowers,
Youth sighed 'Which rose make ours,
Which lily leave and then as best recall?'
Not that, admiring stars,
It yearned 'Nor Jove, nor Mars;
Mine be some figured flame which blends, transcends them all!'

Not for such hopes and fears
Annulling youth's brief years,
Do I remonstrate: folly wide the mark!
Rather I prize the doubt
Low kinds exist without,
Finished and finite clods, untroubled by a spark.

Poor vaunt of life indeed,
Were man but formed to feed
On joy, to solely seek and find and feast:
Such feasting ended, then
As sure an end to men;
Irks care the crop-full bird? Frets doubt the maw-crammed beast?

[272] Robert Browning (1812-1889) "RABBI BEN EZRA" *English Poetry (1170-1892)*: 495. Compiled by John Matthews Manley.

Rejoice we are allied
To That which doth provide
And not partake, effect and not receive!
A spark disturbs our clod;
Nearer we hold of God
Who gives, than of His tribes that take, I must believe.

Then, welcome each rebuff
That turns earth's smoothness rough,
Each sting that bids nor sit nor stand but go!
Be our joys three-parts pain!
Strive, and hold cheap the strain;
Learn, nor account the pang; dare, never grudge the throe!

For thence,—a paradox
Which comforts while it mocks,—
Shall life succeed in that it seems to fail:
What I aspired to be,
And was not, comforts me:
A brute I might have been, but would not sink i' the scale.

What is he but a brute
Whose flesh has soul to suit,
Whose spirit works lest arms and legs want play?
To man, propose this test—
Thy body at its best,
How far can that project thy soul on its lone way?

Yet gifts should prove their use:
I own the Past profuse
Of power each side, perfection every turn:
Eyes, ears took in their dole,
Brain treasured up the whole;
Should not the heart beat once 'How good to live and learn?'

Not once beat 'Praise be Thine!
I see the whole design,
I, who saw power, see now love perfect too:
Perfect I call Thy plan:
Thanks that I was a man!
Maker, remake, complete,—I trust what Thou shalt do!'

For pleasant is this flesh;
Our soul, in its rose-mesh
Pulled ever to the earth, still yearns for rest;
Would we some prize might hold
To match those manifold
Possessions of the brute,—gain most, as we did best!

Let us not always say,
'Spite of this flesh to-day
I strove, made head, gained ground upon the whole!'
As the bird wings and sings,
Let us cry 'All good things
Are ours, nor soul helps flesh more, now, than flesh helps soul!'

Therefore I summon age
To grant youth's heritage,
Life's struggle having so far reached its term:
Thence shall I pass, approved
A man, for aye removed
From the developed brute; a god though in the germ.

And I shall thereupon
Take rest, ere I be gone
Once more on my adventure brave and new:
Fearless and unperplexed,
When I wage battle next,
What weapons to select, what armour to indue.

Youth ended, I shall try
My gain or loss thereby;
Leave the fire ashes, what survives is gold:
And I shall weigh the same,
Give life its praise or blame:
Young, all lay in dispute; I shall know, being old.

For note, when evening shuts,
A certain moment cuts
The deed off, calls the glory from the grey:
A whisper from the west
Shoots—'Add this to the rest,
Take it and try its worth: here dies another day.'

So, still within this life,
Though lifted o'er its strife,
Let me discern, compare, pronounce at last,
This rage was right I' the main,
That acquiescence vain:
The Future I may face now I have proved the Past.'

For more is not reserved
To man, with soul just nerved
To act to-morrow what he learns to-day:
Here, work enough to watch
The Master work, and catch
Hints of the proper craft, tricks of the tool's true play.

As it was better, youth
Should strive, through acts uncouth,
Toward making, than repose on aught found made:
So, better, age, exempt
From strife, should know, than tempt
Further. Thou waitedst age: wait death nor be afraid!

Enough now, if the Right
And Good and Infinite
Be named here, as thou callest thy hand thine own
With knowledge absolute,
Subject to no dispute
From fools that crowded youth, nor let thee feel alone.

Be there, for once and all,
Severed great minds from small,
Announced to each his station in the Past!
Was I, the world arraigned,
Were they, my soul disdained,
Right? Let age speak the truth and give us peace at last!

Now, who shall arbitrate?
Ten men love what I hate,
Shun what I follow, slight what I receive;
Ten, who in ears and eyes
Match me: we all surmise,
They this thing, and I that: whom shall my soul believe?

Not on the vulgar mass
Called 'work,' must sentence pass,
Things done, that took the eye and had the price;
O'er which, from level stand,
The low world laid its hand,
Found straightway to its mind, could value in a trice:

But all, the world's coarse thumb
And finger failed to plumb,
So passed in making up the main account;
All instincts immature,
All purposes unsure,
That weighed not as his work, yet swelled the man's amount:

Thoughts hardly to be packed
Into a narrow act,
Fancies that broke through language and escaped;
All I could never be,
All, men ignored in me,
This, I was worth to God, whose wheel the pitcher shaped.

Ay, note that Potter's wheel,
That metaphor! and feel
Why time spins fast, why passive lies our clay,—
Thou, to whom fools propound,
When the wine makes its round,
'Since life fleets, all is change; the Past gone, seize to-day!'

Fool! All that is, at all,
Lasts ever, past recall;
Earth changes, but thy soul and God stand sure:
What entered into thee,
That was, is, and shall be:
Time's wheel runs back or stops: Potter and clay endure.

He fixed thee mid this dance
Of plastic circumstance,
This Present, thou, forsooth, wouldst fain arrest:
Machinery just meant
To give thy soul its bent,
Try thee and turn thee forth, sufficiently impressed.

What though the earlier grooves,
Which ran the laughing loves
Around thy base, no longer pause and press?
What though, about thy rim,
Skull-things in order grim
Grow out, in graver mood, obey the sterner stress?

Look not thou down but up!
To uses of a cup,
The festal board, lamp's flash and trumpet's peal,
The new wine's foaming flow,
The Master's lips a-glow!
Thou, heaven's consummate cup, what need'st thou with earth's wheel?

But I need, now as then,
Thee, God, who mouldest men;
And since, not even while the whirl was worst,
Did I,—to the wheel of life
With shapes and colours rife,
Bound dizzily,—mistake my end, to slake Thy thirst:

So, take and use Thy work:
Amend what flaws may lurk,
What strain o' the stuff, what warpings past the aim!
My times be in Thy hand!
Perfect the cup as planned!
Let age approve of youth, and death complete the same!

CPSIA information can be obtained
at www.ICGtesting.com
Printed in the USA
BVHW032057240420
578404BV00001B/63